Walk-Ons
ARE WELCOME

The story of a south Georgia farm boy and
Georgia Bulldog and his journey with Jesus Christ

a memoir by BUCK SWINDLE

Published by

. . . . .

FIVE POINTS PRESS
ATHENS, GEORGIA

Five Points Press

500 North Milledge Avenue

Suite 200

Athens, Georgia 30601

706-534-9270

www.fivepointspress.com

Copyright 2011 by Buck Swindle

First Printing

ISBN 978-0-9836834-3-8

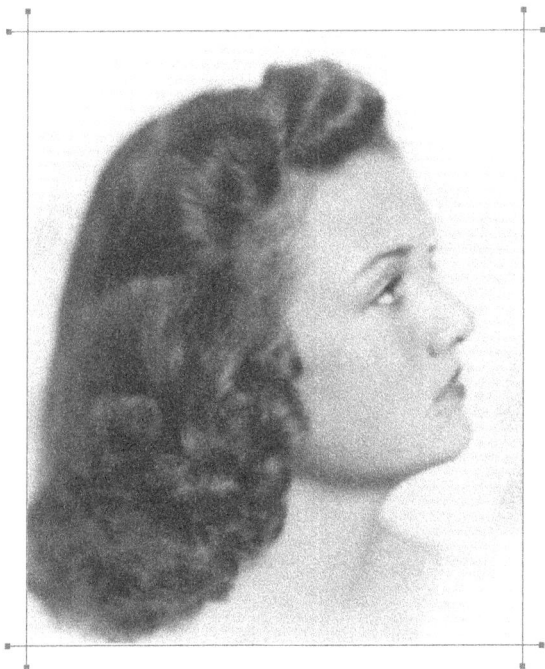

Dedicated to my mother

Betty Patten Swindle

Pictured on the cover is Buck Swindle returning a punt 76 yards in a game against the University of Kentucky at Sanford Stadium during his junior season in 1969.

CONTENTS

FOREWORD

Papa James told me one summer night on the front porch of our home at the Rolling Green Farm in Ray City, Georgia that the most important question parents must ask themselves is what kind of legacy they left for their children. I think at the time I considered the legacy he mentioned in terms of money, land, and other material things. It was some time later in my life that I came to realize that the legacy he was talking about that summer evening was far different than what I had envisioned.

The original purpose for writing this memoir was to provide a written account of my life for my children and grandchildren. As I proceeded with the project over a seven-year period of time, several other purposes of this writing became evident to me. It was like I was being nudged along page by page, tape by tape, to reach a conclusion. Most of the book was written in the early morning hours during the most difficult financial time in my life. It was like someone had directly asked me to document my past and make the experiences available to all.

> It was some time later in my life that I came to realize that the legacy he was talking about that summer evening was far different than what I had envisioned.

Most of my life has been filled with the pursuit of "things" and the preoccupation with "my agenda" first. For most of my life I did not consider God and Jesus Christ as non-existent. I just was too busy to get involved, and through apathy and self-indulgence, I went through life drifting from one materialistic goal to another. I am sure this book is a form of a confession and testimony for me as well. I also know it has been therapeutic for me to hunt and peck my way through these 200+ pages.

As the book progressed, several other new and exciting purposes evolved. I wanted this book to be enjoyable and entertaining, so I added humor and some "down home tales." I wanted the book to provide guidance and advice, especially to younger readers, which is why the 29 heads up points were created and incorporated into this chronicle of my life.

I am hopeful all the above purposes will be achieved, but the most important purpose is to create a real life account of my experience in a personal Christian conversion I didn't think I wanted or needed.

This is the legacy Papa James was talking about on the front porch.

Proceeds from this project will be donated to Carrollton First United Methodist Church Mission Outreach, International Leadership Institute, and Victory Methodist Mission Outreach.

Buck Swindle

I

Early Years:
Life on the Farm

On May 14, 1948, a major event in world history occurred when the Jewish Agency in the Palestine Territory proclaimed independence and named the new country Israel.

On the same day, a half-world away, at Archbold Memorial Hospital in Thomasville, Georgia, another memorable event occurred. It may not have made the front page of newspapers around the globe, but it was nonetheless very important to me. May 14, 1948 was the day of my birth. The son of Harry and Betty Patten Clark, I was named Harry Glen Clark, Jr. after my father.

My parents divorced in early 1952. I was four years old, and my sister Diane was five. My mother moved her two small children, just 17 months apart in age, to Valdosta, and took a job at a local radio station. Although I have a vague recollection of my

The earliest known photo of me, at 4 months, with my Grandmother, Mimi Pat (Clyde Purcell Patten, Bee's mother) and sister Diane.

very early childhood in Thomasville, I clearly remember the apartment that the three of us shared on North Ashley Street beginning in the spring of 1952.

Like most people, my memories prior to school age tend to be vague and limited. However, when my mother, Bee, a nickname that she gave herself, began dating someone, I was old enough to remember and to realize that our lives were about to change forever.

PAPA JAMES CAME INTO OUR LIVES

During those days in Valdosta it was business as usual. Bee was happy working at the radio station, and Diane and I had our school routines in place. However, our now comfortable routines were about to be side tracked when a man named James Swindle came into our lives.

One evening in 1953, Bee explained to Diane and me that the next day we were going to have a sitter because she had a date with a local farmer from Ray City. It was not up for discussion or a vote; she had made up her mind. Bee has always had a keen ability to make simple, clear decisions and stick with them. Diane and I were not pleased with the news, but we said okay and cooperated.

James Swindle came to the door, bearing gifts. Wrigley's Juicy Fruit Gum— what child could turn that down? I was on his team from that point on. I was a huge Juicy Fruit fan, and, undoubtedly, Bee had shared that information with him before he made it to the door for the first time.

Bee and Papa James dated for several months, and before each date, a pack of Juicy Fruit was presented to us as soon as the door was opened. I was always positioned in a winged back chair in our apartment awaiting his arrival. The Wrigley's was sure to follow.

I barely remember when my parents divorced. My mother said something to the effect, "Let's sit down and have a talk." But I clearly remember the moment that my mother once again gathered us together for a talk. This time, because of the serious nature of the issue, there was a democratic process. The decision we were asked to make would surely change my life forever. The vote was unanimous: Bee and Papa James were to be married on Feb. 21, 1954 at the First Presbyterian Church in Waycross, Georgia. Bee was and is a devoted Presbyterian.

Soon after the "vote" on their future marriage, the lease on my mother's apartment was due for renewal. Bee and Papa James decided not to renew the lease and accepted an invitation from Papa James's parents, J. H. and Estelle Swindle, to live with them in Ray City until a tenant farmhouse could be remodeled.

The lifetime relationship I had with Pop began then, even before Bee and Papa James were married. We bonded during long rides around the farm. Those times were filled with great conversations that would influence me throughout my life.

LIVING WITH BIG DADDY AND NANNY

I have vivid memories of living in Ray City with Papa James's parents, affectionately called Big Daddy and Nanny. They exemplified the American spirit.

Big Daddy was a large man with strong hands. He loved the people of Ray City. He was a successful businessman, but in some cases when economic times were tough he did not get paid on debts owed to him. I now have a better understanding of how that must have felt.

The owner of a fancy, bright red pickup with "3 on the column," a three-speed straight shift with the gear switch on the steering column, Big Daddy also had the distinction of owning the first Model T Ford in Ray City.

Big Daddy took me out to the farm, where we visited with the "hands," as most people in the area referred to farm laborers. He never liked that term; Big Daddy preferred "helper." He considered himself a "helper" as well and liked the concept of "we all help each other in our own special way." Big Daddy died in 1954, one of the worst years in Georgia agricultural history.

Nanny was the family matriarch. She was a member of a small Primitive Baptist church in Adel, Georgia, and was the family's spiritual leader. I went to church with her in the summer and was given a paper fan at the door. The church had no electric fans, much less air conditioning. The temperature had to be well over 100 degrees. There was no music during the service, just fire and brimstone preaching.

Nanny was the "Cook of all Cooks," and chicken pie was her specialty. She concocted her recipe in a huge wooden bowl with crust all around the sides. Her bowl now holds a place of honor in the center of our kitchen table. She also supervised the annual "Corn Day." When the fall crops came in, we formed an assembly line to process the silver queen corn. The entire family was involved, each person with a specific job. I

From left to right, Big Daddy, Papa James, and Nanny in 1942.

was the designated shucker. "Corn Day" was usually an all-day Saturday event. It was tough work, but it all seemed worthwhile on frosty January days when we ate corn that tasted fresh from the field.

Nanny was a great lady. It was a sad day when Pop called and told me that she had retired to Heaven. It is strange sometimes the things that you remember. I was having dinner at Bennie's Red Barn in St. Simons when I got Papa James's call.

During the engagement, Papa James and his Uncle Razzee Swindle, an astute and meticulous carpenter, began remodeling one of the six old tenant houses on the farm that had been inhabited by sharecropper families in the 30s and 40s. Pop and Bee selected the house that was in the best shape and could be easily converted to a three-bedroom floor plan.

The goal was to have the house ready by their wedding day. We were to move in after the honeymoon.

Everything looked good initially, but there were a couple of problems: January weather and Uncle Razzee. The weather was extremely cold, and Uncle Razzee just did not get in a hurry. Papa James was a perfectionist, but he liked to speed things along. Uncle Razzee was a perfectionist, and he moved at a deliberate pace.

One of Bee's many attributes has always been her attention to detail. She often said, "If you do the simple things well, then good, big things will follow." She and Uncle Razzee got sideways on some "Oh by the way, can we add this?" suggestions.

Between Pop pressing the deadline and Bee's personal additions we were on the verge of losing the best carpenter in Berrien County. I replaced Papa James as carpenter apprentice. Since Papa James was busy on the farm he was happy to turn the job over to me and let Uncle Razzee take charge.

One particular aspect of the farmhouse renovation that I will always remember was the discussion about the strength of the hinges for the front door and windows. Uncle Razzee wanted to use a heavy duty door with large, commercial-style hinges. After some hesitation because of the additional cost, Papa James agreed to the more expensive, upgraded door and window fixtures. This decision had a major impact on the outcome of a life threatening experience eight years later.

The house was finished a month after the February wedding, and we moved in March of 1954.

MOVING TO THE FARM AND THE GREAT DROUGHT

Although we were happy to live on the farm full-time, the region was in the midst of a great drought that was setting all-time records. There was no irrigation, and farming was a gamble. Thank God, Bee was offered an excellent job as a purchasing agent at nearby Moody Air Force Base in Valdosta. I am not sure we would have survived financially that first year without her employment.

During her 26 years at Moody, Bee worked her way up to one of the highest GS ratings for females in the civil service sector. Our family will always be grateful to those who worked tirelessly to sustain and advance Moody Field as a viable part or our defense system today.

On the farm, we lived on an intersection of two dirt roads, Georgia

Highway 122 and Swindle Road. There was very little traffic, and except for the dust, our quality of life was far better with dirt roads than when they were later paved. In rural South Georgia, a common misconception was that homes on dirt roads were those of "lower class people" with limited means. Pop actually opposed the paving of Highway 122. He was sure that with a layer of asphalt, he would soon have South Georgia's version of the Talladega racetrack in his own front yard. He was right.

My sister, Diane, and I settled into farm life, but it was different in many ways. We were enrolled at Pine Grove Elementary School in downtown Bemis, Georgia, eight miles south of the farm. The four buses that provided transportation for the Pine Grove students had a unique identification system. On each side of the door was a Disney character. Since I was a huge fan of the Mickey Mouse Club, I was really excited that I would ride the "Mickey Bus." There were also Donald Duck, Pluto and Popeye the Sailor Man buses.

Every day after school, I would turn on our black and white TV and adjust the foil-wrapped rabbit ear antennae to sharpen the reception. I put on my black felt Mouseketeer ears, and promptly at 5:30, I would sing the "Mickey Mouse Club" theme song along with an entire nation of 7-year-olds. It was a simple and happy time in my childhood.

During the years on Rolling Green Farm, our family tried several farm-related business ventures. One that I distinctly remember was the hog parlor. The facility was located on the southern end of the farm and was built shortly after we moved to the farm house that Uncle Razzee remodeled. It was a "state of the art" facility with heat lamps and all the works to protect the new born piglets during the winter. We bred Spotted Poland China hogs. They were docile and were marked with a big ring around their middles.

South Georgia winters were tough, especially if you were in the hog breeding business. The sows were bred to deliver in late winter to early spring, but some came early during the worst period of the winter. Some mothers would give birth and decide to devour their babies. It was gruesome, but a fact nevertheless.

I went to the hog parlor with Papa James to watch as the babies were born. We put them in a cardboard box, took them back to the house, and put the box in front of the gas heater. We fed them until they could nurse on their own; this also seemed to be the point when the piglets were no longer in danger of consumption by the sow.

Following the second year of operation Papa James sold the hogs and closed the hog operation.

RIDING AND TALKING WITH PAPA JAMES

Papa James and I continued our routine rides around the farm, and we could always find something to talk about. There were no cell phones, computers, or other electronic distractions. Life was simple and fulfilling. The farm was our life.

Papa James placed a high priority on helping others, and farm life allowed him to be generous without sacrificing someone else's pride. He loved to see the crops "come in," and was always giving someone a "mess" of something. He had a knack for cultivation and growing, but he also had some of the most fertile land with which to work. The sandy loam soil was ideal for growing just about anything, and as we drove he explained the importance of the underground river called the aquifer. There was never a problem digging a deep water well, and the water was always fresh and clean.

On those countless trips, Papa James and I would frequent certain well-known local hot spots like the Victory Soda Shop in downtown Ray City. Considered a landmark in those days, the Vicotry Soda shop was once mentioned by well-known sports columnist Furman Bisher after I signed with the Georgia Bulldogs. Located on a corner block in the center of town, it was the hub of all social activity in Ray City. You could enter from either side of the corner.

There were wooden benches outside each entrance. Lettered clearly across the bench facing Main Street were the words, "White Only." The bench on the other side was labeled "Colored." I never sat on either of the benches. If you walk down that sidewalk today on the Main Street side of the soda shop you will still see a granite block inscribed with Big Daddy's name, J.H. Swindle.

Billy Clements sold a wide variety of items in the Victory Soda Shop, including handmade sodas, the best bitter-sweet lemonade, and the tastiest, greasiest hamburgers on the planet. He also sold, of all things in a soda shop, fish bait. Occasionally, Billy would get in a hurry and go from scooping night crawlers to spreading mayo on a hamburger without stopping to wash his hands. Papa James was a big believer in washing one's hands. Cleanliness was indeed next to godliness, and Pop never failed to remind Billy, especially when his burger was in hand.

Another well-known establishment in the area was the Silver Dollar, which was located on the Lakeland-Ray City Highway about half way to Lakeland. I never actually went inside, but we did make a few stops there over the years. Prior to the construction of I-75, all of the north-south traffic was on Georgia 41, and the Silver Dollar was not far from that highway. During the annual Georgia-Florida Week prior to the Bulldogs-Gators game in Jacksonville, the Silver Dollar did a landslide business as a watering hole and supplier of various to-go libations.

THE FIGHT IN TALLAHASSEE

Although Papa James never started a fight— at least not when I was with him— he was not afraid to defend himself and his family when necessary. One such encounter happened on a Saturday night in Tallahassee, Florida. I was a sophomore in high school. We made the 60 mile drive to Tallahassee to see the University of Georgia play Florida State University in a night game at Doak Campbell Stadium. It was 1964, Coach Vince Dooley's first year as Georgia's head football coach. FSU featured Fred Biletnikoff, one of the greatest wide receivers to ever play the game, and all-star quarterback Steve Tensi. The Seminoles were nationally ranked, and UGA was an up-and-coming power. At that time I had no idea I would later play for the Bulldogs. I was actually a Georgia Tech and Florida fan at the time.

In that game one of my future coaches, Bob Taylor, suffered a broken leg and was lost for the season. Bob remains a great Bulldog legacy. He was the player who took the pitch from Pat Hodgson on the famous flea-flicker play after Pat caught a pass from Georgia's quarterback Kirby Moore. Bob ran 73 yards for a touchdown to beat Bear Bryant's national champion Crimson Tide in 1965.

On this night in Tallahassee following Florida State's win over the Bulldogs, we headed for a postgame dinner. Papa James, Bee, "Uncle Jim" Paulk, his date, and I went to a "5-Star" steak house on the outskirts of Tallahassee.

Uncle Jim was a cousin and great friend of Papa James. He owned Del-Cook Lumber Company in Adel, Georgia and was a successful businessman. Papa James attempted for many years to bring Christ into Uncle Jim's life. I'm not sure he was ever successful, but before Uncle Jim died, he did ask God to forgive him. Pop said that he made it just in time.

The steak house held at least 150 people, and it was packed after the game. The five of us were seated at a table in the back. In the booth next to us were two young, strong-looking guys. Papa James liked his steak to come to the table with "a little moo still in it." Just knock the horns off and run it through the kitchen. When Pop's steak arrived "done to a cracklin," he immediately, but politely, asked the waitress to have another one cooked. Our waitress was fine with returning the charred steak to the kitchen, but one of the young men in the adjacent booth decided to make our business his business. He made a serious mistake, when he sarcastically offered to buy "the son of a bitch a steak if he's not satisfied." Without saying a word, Papa James got up, walked over to the man who was half his age and twice his size, grabbed him by his collar, stood him up against the wall, and punched him three or four times before he even knew what hit him. Blood splattered the back wall of the booth like a ripe tomato thrown by an Atlanta Braves's best closer.

Papa James got carried away and kept hitting the guy until I got on his back and pulled him off. As chaotic as the situation had become, I was amazed at how Bee remained so calm. She told me to get Papa James outside while she went for the car, and that we would take care of the incident later. Bee was in total control of the situation. She brought the car around, and once in, we headed for home. By the time we dropped Uncle Jim and his date off and returned home, it was one o'clock in the morning. We gathered around the pine log table and prayed. Papa James asked for forgiveness. We later paid for the minor damages and our uneaten meals and moved on with our lives.

Sister Diane (left) and I are pictured with a friend, waiting for Mr. Hunter's school bus.

THE CHRISTMAS TREE

As a young boy growing up in rural Georgia on a farm, miles from the nearest town, I learned to be innovative when I needed transportation or needed to transport other things, like maybe a Christmas tree.

On our farm, there was an abundance of beautiful cedar trees. At Christmas time we always cut our own, so when my fifth grade teacher asked for a volunteer to provide a Christmas tree for our classroom, I just assumed it would be no problem. Wrong! The tree itself was not the problem; it was how to get it to school. Since I had not asked Papa James in advance about taking the tree to school, and since it needed to be there the next day, he said that he would cut it and bring it to the yard, but it was up to me to get it to school. He cut the tree and unloaded it next to the dirt road going south toward school. I had to think of something in a hurry. I had an idea.

Mr. Hunter was our bus driver on the "Mickey Bus." He was also our milk man and family friend. He delivered milk to our house every other day. I would wait at the edge of the yard, and when the bus pulled up I would take the milk, run inside, put it in the refrigerator, and run back to get on the bus. Every Friday, I was in charge of paying him for the milk.

On this particular day just before Christmas holidays, I think I tried Mr. Hunter's patience. When he pulled in to deliver the milk and pick me up, I explained to him that I needed to get the tree to school. To say that he was a bit testy would be an understatement. When he realized that I wanted him to tie the tree to the side of the bus he said that there was no way he could haul a tree that big. I told him that I had a rope, and pleaded with him to help me. He said, "No way!"

I wouldn't take no for an answer. I kept begging, and he finally gave in. Mr. Hunter was my hero that day as the "Mickey Bus" pulled into Pine Grove School with a Christmas tree strapped to its side. We had a grand Christmas party that year, and Bee and Papa James came to see our beautifully decorated tree. (Mr. Hunter did call me off to the side that day and made sure that we had a complete understanding regarding future bus policies.) I was so proud of that tree.

THE TOBACCO PATCH

As I began to get older, I was asked to do more work on the farm. I was doing well academically at Pine Grove and played basketball at the junior high level. I really wanted to play football, but most of my time after school was devoted to farm work. Papa James was working day and night to keep the farm going, and Bee was working at Moody Air Force Base as well as doing domestic work at home.

Tobacco was a major part of the South Georgia economy. Most farms had a tobacco allotment for a certain amount of acreage and poundage of tobacco that could be marketed from that particular farm each year. No doubt tobacco paid the bills on the farm in those days, but the work necessary to produce flue cured tobacco was beyond description. Once the plants went in the ground in the late spring, it was 24/7.

We had twelve flue-cured, pole-constructed tobacco barns with fuel-fired burners. Each barn was approximately 16' x 16' square and 30' tall with ventilation at the top and sides, and was made from pine logs. Inside were poles spaced every 8 to 10 feet.

Tobacco farming defined high maintenance. One of the most laborious and nastiest jobs was "topping and suckering." The process, very simply, involved moving along a row of tobacco that was as long as you could see, picking the "sucker" leaves out from between the primary leaf and the main stalk, and dropping them on the ground. It also required breaking the top out of each plant toward the end of the growing season. After a day of suckering, it was nearly impossible to remove the gum from your hands and body. Throughout my life and of all the jobs I have tried along the way, suckering tobacco will go down as the one I hated most.

When the tobacco plants were three to four feet tall, it was time to make the first harvest which was called "cropping sand lugs." This required an entire workday of walking down the rows of tobacco, bending at the waist, and picking the bottom leaves. These leaves were of the poorest quality, but they still needed to be harvested to make room for the more valuable cigarette leaves near the top of the plants. Cropping sand lugs on foot in 100 degree heat was beyond tough.

I was never allowed to take part in this particular process because of the ever-present danger of running across a rattlesnake looking for mid-day shade. It was just a matter of time until they would sing those rattles. The field guys were savvy, and most of them could hear rattlers two or three plants ahead. They would stop and wait while the deadly snake moved on, or they would, in one swift, efficient motion, chop him in half. Diamondbacks were so common that it was no big deal, and seldom did a worker get bitten. Papa James could kill a rattler with a six-inch adjustable wrench.

We later bought a mechanical tobacco harvester, which eliminated the walking and the back-bending. However, because it was so much faster, the rattlers became more of a threat. The harvester's seats were just 18 inches from the ground and the operators had to be lightning quick to make production. Consequently, the workers had no advance warning until one of them was bitten.

As the harvester moved down the row, the croppers attached four to five main leaves on a conveyor that were transported to the stringer. The stringer took the clumps of leaves off the conveyor sections and strung

My grandmother, Estelle "Nanny" Swindle (top left) and grandfather, J.H. "Big Daddy" Swindle stand in his prime tobacco crop in the summer of 1925 with my aunts, Doris and Grace Swindle, and James A. "Papa James" Swindle.

each bundle on either side of a heart pine tobacco stick. Stringing was a unique skill and had to be done with precision. If the string was too tight, it would cut through the tender leaves' stalks, or if too loose, the leaves would fall off. The process required careful monitoring, and was therefore a high paying job.

Once the sticks were full of tobacco on each side, I took them from the stringer, stacked them on a pallet, and handed him an empty stick for the next round.

Harvesting tobacco mechanically required 10 to 12 workers. Once we had a full load of cigarette-grade tobacco pallets we headed to the flue-cured pole barns. Since I was tall and long legged I met the requirements of a "barn hanger."

The inside poles were approximately six feet wide and six feet high and extended to the top of the barn's vented roof. The tobacco was hung green in the barn where it cured. After curing, it was taken down and removed stick-by-stick for disassembly and storage in burlap. For three years I hung tobacco sticks in all 12 barns. But when I was 16 years old, things changed.

THE NOISE YOU WILL ALWAYS KNOW

I had completed most of a routine takedown in one particular barn. The sticks were blocking the sunlight, and I could barely see. I removed the sticks by feel. I was counting each level of poles and knew that I was near the top and would soon break into the light.

Suddenly, I heard the noise that anyone who has worked in tobacco immediately recognizes. It was a distinct rattle, but I had no idea where he was. My head was near the top of the barn, and the sound seemed near my ear. Workers regularly survived a bite to the hand or leg, but to the head or neck was usually fatal. I didn't hesitate to let go.

As I fell, I hit both guys below me, and we ended up in a pile at the bottom of the barn. I was the color of cotton and shaking like a leaf. The older guys started laughing and insisted that "there is no way a rattler is up that high. No way!"

Papa James came by later and asked the guys to take a light and climb the poles to see what they thought. They were hesitant to enter the dark barn, and it was obvious that they no longer were sure that snakes can't climb.

HEADS UP #1

Miracles happen

- Know God's examples of miracles: creation, birth, our bodies, healings, and Jesus' miracle ministry.

- Miracles are everywhere

- Never underestimate the power of prayer.

After six days Jesus took with him Peter, James and John, the brother of James, and led them to a high mountain by themselves. There he was transfigured before them. His face shone like the sun, and his clothes became white as light.

– Matthew 17:1-3

With the "assistance" of a 20-gauge Model 12 shotgun, they brought down a rattlesnake that was just under six feet in length with 15 rattles and a button. The snake was wrapped around the very next pole I was about to unload. We estimated that this "bad boy" had been about two feet away from my right ear. That day I retired from hanging tobacco.

Sometime after that memorable season, Papa James announced one night at the dinner table that he had sold his tobacco allotment. It was one of my happier days. Praise God.

The 1961 Pony League Berrien Giants were coached by Papa James (top row, left), Judge W.D. "Jack" Knight, and John David Luke. I am sitting on the first row, third from the left.

THE PONY LEAGUE BASEBALL EXPERIENCE

Papa James had been an outstanding athlete, and I wanted to follow in his footsteps. It was 1960 when he brought Little League baseball to Berrien County. Pop, John David Luke, and Judge W.D. "Jack" Knight sponsored our team.

I was 12 years old and was ecstatic when Pop told me that a four-team league was being formed in Nashville. Because of my age, I would only be eligible to play for one year. At that time I had only played sandlot ball, but it didn't matter to me; I was a Cardinal and was sporting the #12. I did okay, but Papa James wanted me to shine.

The following year in 1961 Pop rented out the farm and consequently had more free time. He and the same sponsors formed a team that competed in the Pony League program in Tifton, Georgia. Looking back, it's hard to believe that we did what we did. We lived 46 miles from Tifton. The sponsors bought a bus, and with Pop and our other two coaches, we made the 92 mile round trip two to three times a week for the entire summer season.

It was fun at first, but quickly began to wear on all of us. I was a wreck. The speed of the game was beyond my ability, and I couldn't hit my way out of a wet paper bag. We lost and traveled and lost and traveled some more. I was really getting burned out. It was probably one of the few times, if not the only time, my relationship with Papa James was strained.

The Tifton Pony League season finally came to an end. Pop and I agreed that it just did not work out. He decided not to rent out the farm again and went back to doing what he enjoyed— farming and raising cattle.

I didn't feel right about what happened. I felt like I had let Pop down. He had made obvious sacrifices just so I could play organized baseball. Renting out the farm had given him time to be personally involved. I knew he had done it for me, and it was tearing me up inside. I wanted to do something to make it right, to make it up to him. I had a year to think it over. The Pony League baseball season of the summer of 1961 was forgotten, and I didn't play ball during the summer of 1962. Instead I worked in the hay field and for the county tax assessor's office.

HAVING FUN IN COLT LEAGUE BASEBALL

As it turned out, I made some connections with a few guys I knew from Valdosta. They played organized summer baseball at the Valdosta Boy's Club. It was an ongoing Colt League and was first class. The pitching mound was 15 feet further back than it had been at Pony League, and seemed more "user-friendly" for a sub .200 hitter with a phobia of fast balls coming from the mound like aspirin tablets.

In the spring of 1963, I went to Papa James and asked him if I could play summer Colt League baseball in Valdosta. Although he knew nothing about the program, Pop said that he would get me to the games but would not be directly involved with the team.

I later learned that Papa James regretted pushing me so hard during the Pony League season in '61. We had been inseparable and the absolute best of friends. We were involved with each other to some degree every day, and were putting excessive pressure on each other; it was time for some needed separation. Even now it is difficult to admit that we were really too close for our own good in those days.

I played for the Auto Dealers of Valdosta Colt League team that had a 16 game schedule. Pop dropped me off and picked me up after practice and games, which was no big deal compared to the 92 mile round trip to and from Tifton two summers before.

Prior to beginning Colt League play I made up my mind that I was not going to step out of the batter's box on speed. I resolved to step in instead, and I didn't care if I got hit. There were no more tentative swings. I wanted to have fun.

Soon after starting practice with the team, Pop casually asked how it was going. I told him that I had made the starting team. I sensed his pride, since Colt League was for 15-, 16-, and 17-year-olds, and I had just turned 15 a few months earlier. I was more aggressive at the plate and the aspirin tablets that had intimidated me two summers ago had been reduced to moth balls. It was fun.

LIGHTNING AND FIRE ON THE FENCE LINE

It was a typical South Georgia summer evening: hot and humid. We had a 7:30 p.m. game in Valdosta, and I was scheduled to start at second base and bat leadoff. We were leading the league, and I was batting over .300. But I never told Pop. He had not seen a single game.

It was about 5:30 p.m., and I was dressed in my white with blue trim Auto Owners # 10 jersey and pants. Papa James and I were riding and looking over things at the farm before the trip to the game when we noticed a huge, black cloud to the south with a vibrant red glow. It was the sign of a farmer's nightmare: hail and severe lightning!

In a matter of minutes the sky was electrified. It was lightning like I had never seen, but there was no rain. We just pulled over and watched. It was strange. No rain and all this lightning. We heard a loud clap of lightning on the north end of the farm and immediately noticed smoke on the shoulder of the road. Pop said that it was fire!

I looked in the opposite direction and saw more smoke. All of a sudden there were several fires along the fence line. Lightning had struck the fence and everywhere dry grass was touching the fence a fire erupted.

Papa James jumped out of the truck and said, "Cut a pine top and go south, and I will go north. Now!"

There was no time to waste! The fires were small at first, but there were so many, and there was only the two of us. It was a miracle that we had not left for the game earlier as we had done many times before. If we had left directly for Valdosta there is no doubt that the family farm timber would have been destroyed.

We fought the fires for over an hour, but they kept coming back. Then a miracle occurred when it started to rain. We called the county fire department, and they came out, cut fire breaks, and got the situation under control.

Pop and I were exhausted. I was covered in soot and had a large burn hole in the left knee of my baseball pants. Thank goodness we had no physical burns.

I had no idea that we would still go to Valdosta for the game. Papa James said, "We have the county on scene now. Maybe there is a rain delay at the game. Let's go check it out."

So we took off for the ballpark in Valdosta. Papa James had not seen me play a Colt League game all season.

When we arrived, sure enough there had been a delay, but the game was in the middle of the fourth inning. I believe the score was tied. Obviously, my position had been taken, so I just sat on the bench in a soot-covered, burned uniform. Although Papa James dropped me off and said that he would be back later, I had a feeling that he was watching from somewhere.

The game was close all the way and tied again in the bottom of the seventh, the last inning of regulation. We had a guy on first with one out when the coach asked me to pinch hit. I hit the first pitch in the gap in left center. The guy on first circled the bases and slid in head first at home, and the game was over. After packing up we went to the Krystal across the street and ate all the minis they had. What a day! Thank God for the rain and a miracle.

I played Colt League baseball in Valdosta for the next two summers and made the Colt League All-Star Team my last year. We lost the state championship by one game in the finals in Rome that season. In that championship game, I played against Charles Whittemore, who would be a football teammate of mine at the University of Georgia the following year. Charlie and I became good friends and were initiated together in the Pi Kappa Alpha fraternity at University of Georgia.

I also met Glenn "Barnie" Davis, who was a consensus high school All-American at Valdosta High School during that time. Barnie was a highly recruited quarterback and signed with UGA. We became good friends and spent a lot of time on I-75 going to and from Athens during the next four years.

MY FIRST MENTOR AND RIVER FISHING ON THE ALAPAHA

My first real mentor was Preacher Shaw from Ray City, Ga. Preacher was not really a preacher, but the name was hung on him in his earlier days. I think he had paved a "wide path" at one time during his life, but he had definitely settled down when I met him. He was a genuine friend and devoted outdoorsman.

Since Papa James was very busy with the farm and did not have much time to fish, Preacher Shaw taught me everything about fishing. Papa James loved to fish, but he was always on the go. To quote him, he could get a "mess of fish or a mess of fishing" pretty quick. His patience ran a little thin at times, but Pop was good at it when he took the time to go.

Preacher Shaw was retired from occupations unknown to me and loved everything about rural life. He was a great friend of Papa James. We hit it off from the start. I will never forget the first time he asked me to go fishing. I was about seven and was ready to go.

Preacher was much like Uncle Razzee in that he was deliberate and a perfectionist. He showed me how to tie my first knot, how to rig the cane poles and bass rods, and how to clean fish. Preacher took me fishing to our farm ponds and other ponds all over the county. I never understood why every fisherman in South Georgia, including Preacher and Papa James, called a bass a trout and a crappie a speckled perch, but they did.

I really loved fishing, and we had many great trips summer after summer. None of the trips, however, compared to the experiences that we had on the banks of the Alapaha River. River trips were special, and it took confidence, skill and preparation to make it happen. Papa James and Preacher planned the river trips weeks in advance. We would always depart before daybreak and drive together with the boat, tackle, fish cooker, crickets, crawlers, peanut oil, hush puppy mix, onions, slaw and pickles.

We headed to the north end of Berrien County to a spot on the river that was good for boat entry and a suitable campsite where we unloaded our gear. The water was as black as soot, but was clean with a sandy bottom. At this point in the Alapaha the water was not moving very fast so we could maneuver the boat with paddles.

Each of us had a cane pole that was as limber as a willow branch. Preacher and Pop wanted very flexible poles to get the most enjoyment out of catching the challenging south Georgia river red breasted bream. Reddish in color and with a clear, clean underside and a taste that was incredible, river bream were different than pond bream.

River fishing was different than pond fishing. The current was a huge factor, so we had to position the boat to be able to cast our pole sideways to get under the willow branches where the red breasts liked to congregate. Pop kept the paddle in the water most of the time and maneuvered it side-to-side to get us into position. It was tricky, but Pop was great with one hand on the paddle and the other casting.

I fished in the presence of two of the best in presenting the bait to waiting recipients. The key was to time the catch to match the time we needed to eat. Preacher and Pop had it down to a science. I cannot ever remember when we did not catch enough fish at the right time.

After the catch, we cleaned the fish and bagged the by-products carefully. Neither Papa James nor Preacher tolerated littering. Both of them strongly believed in the premise that if you took care of the land and natural resources, the land and natural resources would take care of you.

While the peanut oil was heating up in a deep, cured, cast iron pot, each of us had a task to complete. I cleaned the fish, Pop made the slaw and batter, and Preacher made the hush puppies, his specialty that was somewhat of a secret recipe. When the oil was right, Preacher started frying fish. He would take a sample out and let it cool a minute. We always said a prayer during the cooling process.

The fish and trimmings were always "to die for," and we ate until we could not move. This was the true experience of eating fresh fish.

We would take a brief siesta after the feast while the grease was cooling. Papa James and Preacher always strained and saved the grease for later

HEADS UP #2

Mentoring Matters: Get one and be one

• Mentoring stands for accountability and promotes positive results.

• Find a way to make a difference by becoming a mentor.

• The need and opportunities are everywhere.

But you, man of God, flee from all this, and pursue righteousness, godliness, faith, love, endurance, and gentleness. Fight the good fight for the faith. Take hold of the eternal life to which you were called when you made your good confession in the presence of many witnesses.

– 1 Timothy 6:11-12

use. After packing the boat and gear we headed home. Since we always had plenty of extra fish Pop took fish to elderly and needy people in Ray City on a regular basis.

Alapaha River fishing with Papa James and Preacher Shaw was a special time. I thank God for allowing mentors like Preacher Shaw to come into my life. He taught me so much about life during the many hours on the water that we spent together. Fishing is such a great life lesson teacher. It requires patience and attention to detail and allows you to connect with nature in a unique way. I have made it a priority to spend time fishing with my children.

Recently, fishing provided me with the opportunity to have a special experience and share some Christian man-to-man views with a young man who had experienced some problems. He asked me to take him night crappie fishing on Lake Wedowee. Although I was tired from taking my son the previous night, I agreed, and we rolled out at 3 a.m.

We had a blast, caught 15 nice fish, and talked about "stuff" until daybreak. I think some really good things came out during those early morning hours of dark stillness.

From my childhood experiences growing up in South Georgia, I learned that God expects us to help each other. Mentoring a young person in the same way I had been mentored by Papa James and Preacher Shaw many years ago is a great way to contribute. Everyone is more accountable and inclined to contribute responsibly if they know someone with respect and concern is interacting with them on a regular basis.

HOG KILLING TIME

After the tobacco allotment and corn crop were sold and some bills were paid, we gathered together all of our "worker-friends," as Big Daddy would call them, local neighbors, and family to plan the annual hog killing. We waited for a good frost to stage the activity. It was an event that would attract people from throughout the area.

I had no problem with the first step in the hog killing process that began with a single hollow point .32 round delivered to the correct location on the hog. I also didn't have a problem when the carcass was boiled and the hair scraped off. Neither did I have an issue when the carcass was hung, cut open, and all the insides spilled into a # 2 wash tub.

Where my problem began was when the "chittlin' cookin'" began. For the uninformed, chitterlings, often pronounced as "chittlins" in the vernacular of the South, are the intestines of a pig that are prepared as food.

I could not get within 100 yards of the large black pot in which the chittlins were cooked. I could not understand why some people were not bothered by the smell and how they could stand by the pot and stir the mix with a steel post.

Hog killin' was an all-day affair. In addition to the chittlins, we also processed the hams, ribs, shoulders, sausage, bacon, and lard. I knew about the "Mountain Oysters," the hog's testicles, and avoided them at all costs. I thought I had everything covered, but I was wrong.

There was an "extra" from the hog killin' of which I was not aware until one Sunday evening. We had a tradition on Sunday nights of having a breakfast meal at dinner. One night, Papa James decided to cook, which he did quite often. Pop was a good cook, but he did not understand the concept of low-calorie anything. It was all about freshness and the flavor.

Pop started cooking our Sunday night breakfast, and although the aroma was awesome, it seemed a little different this particular night. We gathered for dinner at our family trademark pine log kitchen table, and Pop served the plates. We had fresh country ham, biscuits, and eggs, or what appeared to be a "type" of eggs. They looked a bit darker than most scrambled eggs but smelled great.

We said thanksgiving and started passing plates. I was about midway through and on my second helping of eggs when I asked Pop what recipe he used for the eggs. They were just so good and different.

"Oh," he said. "It's no big deal. These are not just eggs.
They are brains and eggs! "
I said, "What do you mean! I am eating brains?"
He replied, "No, you already have."

Somehow my appetite just kind of left the scene.

Pop got a chuckle out of that. We joked later about my first experience with hog brains. He explained that the only thing not used from the hog is the "oink." I was very careful in the future about those Sunday "breakfasts."

We also often had what was called "S--- on a Shingle" on Sunday nights. That dish included chopped mystery meat with a cream sauce poured over toast. Actually, it was great!

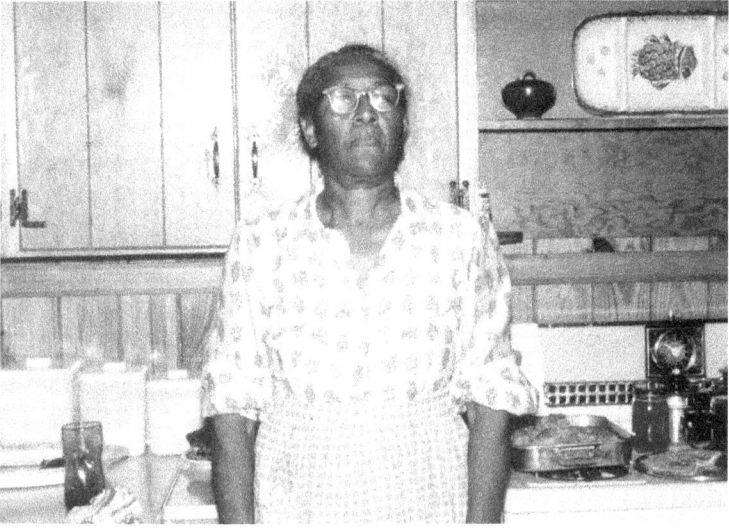

There has never been a finer Christian person who honored God's green earth than Dorcas "Sweet" Shepherd.

SWEET SHEPHERD AND REMER

There has never been a finer Christian person who honored God's green earth than Dorcas "Sweet" Shepherd. Sweet, who came to work for us just after Bee began work at Moody AFB, stayed with us for over 20 years until her retirement when I was in college. She was a mentor, teacher, friend, Bible scholar and was, no doubt, the best cook who ever lived!

Sweet, who lived alone in a small house off a dirt driveway just past Charlie Mac's garage about three miles from our house, came every Wednesday and Saturday. We loved Sweet like our own family. She prayed and sang spiritual songs all day while working. She was never down. The cover of Sweet's Bible was worn to shreds. Many times Bee and Sweet would sit, talk, and read to each other for hours.

At noon on Saturdays, Sweet would prepare a large "dinner," as it was known to south Georgians. Sweet's specialty was a thin cornbread that should have been patented. She used a cast iron skillet that was not more than one inch thick with a thin rim around it. She said it was the skillet that made the hoecake so good. However, I know others who used the same skillet, but didn't get the same results. It was the cook, not the skillet.

My second favorite food that Sweet prepared was fried quail. She fixed fried birds, thin gravy that you poured into a bowl out of your grits, and fresh field peas.

Sweet was born to give, and she did so much for our family. I am sure that she is enjoying someone cooking for her in heaven. Sweet was an incredible lady.

Another loyal friend with a dedicated spirit was Remer. Remer provided any type of yard and landscape duties that were needed. Always dependable and constantly offering to help out in any way he could, Remer worked at a deliberate pace into his 70s. Never one to hesitate in stating his Christian views and personal testimony, Remer would also preach and witness to you when he felt the desire.

PHYSICAL REFERENCES

I am one of those individuals who needs some type of physical reference to keep me in focus. I wear a salvation bracelet given to me by a young girl during a church mission trip we made a few years ago in Mexico at Aleanza Real. It's a daily reminder to be thankful for what I have and not be concerned about what I don't have.

Our church constructed a huge white cross on the outskirts of Carrollton last year which I notice every time I go past it. It reminds me to pray for safety in travel, and it reminds me of all that we have in which to be thankful. The ancient Hebrews were commissioned by God to construct a physical location to honor their Creator. The Ark of the Covenant was created and served as a portable tabernacle for dedication and worship.

Another vivid physical remembrance that I still cherish is an old pine log table that Papa James restained and brought to our farmhouse that Uncle Razzee remodeled in 1954. The table was our forum for eating, decision making, creating, visiting, praying, and whatever project was due the next day at Pine Grove Elementary School. At the time I don't think we realized the importance of the stability that this table represented for our family.

As of this writing, the table remains in excellent condition and sits in my office. Its importance to my family and me came to mind not long ago when I very nearly lost it.

Diane (left) and me 'clowning around' in costumes Bee
made sometime in the fifties.

THE PAULKS AND ROLLING GREEN FARM

Rolling Green Farm was home for 40 years for our family. We lived it.
We breathed it. And we cried with it.

The life lessons learned at Rolling Green Farm are too numerous to
count. The respect that the land commanded made it a pleasure to be a
part of such a fine place. All land belongs to God, and He allows us to
briefly occupy it. I will always be extremely appreciative for being allowed
to be a part of that special land and life many years ago.

The life lessons learned at Rolling Green Farm are too numerous to count. The respect that the land commanded made it a pleasure to be a part of such a fine place.

When Papa James made his trip to eternity, it was time for the farm to change. Life is all about change, and Papa James and I talked about who he wanted to carry on the farm. Papa James and Bee were very fortunate to have great neighbors, Sheriff Ashley Paulk and his wife, Ginger. Ashley and Ginger own the farm today and have done a great job managing not only our farm, but many other surrounding farms. They have made a huge impact on the quality of life for the people of Lowndes County and are dedicated public and private servants.

Special thanks go to the Paulks for all that they did for our family and for all the people who they have positively affected for so many years.

A debt of gratitude is also owed to Brent Stalvey and his family for all they did for us. Brent helped us in many ways and was always available. Brent was the only non-family person to own land within the farm during Papa James's life.

I am very grateful for the legacy and the wonderful standards of life that were set at Rolling Green Farm. We look forward to a continuation of these principles for generations to come.

II
HIGH SCHOOL DAYS
BERRIEN COUNTY HIGH

When I graduated from Pine Grove Elementary in Bemis, Ga. in 1962 I had an option to enroll at Lowndes County High in Valdosta, Hahira High (yes, Hahira had a high school), or Berrien County High School in Nashville, Ga.

Hahira was the closest, being eight miles away from home. Berrien and Lowndes were about 16 miles away. I chose Berrien because Papa James had business relationships in Berrien County, and I thought I had a better chance to make the football team. I had never played organized football before I stepped on to the practice field at Berrien High in the summer of 1962.

I celebrated my fourteenth birthday on May 14, 1962, just prior to 8th grade graduation at Pine Grove. One evening in late April as we gathered around the pine log table in the kitchen, Papa James asked me a simple question. He asked me if I wanted him to adopt me and become his legal son. We had discussed this subject prior to the meeting, and I had made up my mind. I said yes, and I picked my own name, Mark Stephen Swindle.

I want to say that this situation had to be difficult for my father, Harry Clark. I look back on that decision today and often wonder how I would have reacted if I were in his position. I do not regret the decision, but I must say that I appreciate the relationship Daddy and I have had and continue to have to this very day. He has always been supportive of me and willing at all times to be there for me. We have been separated geographically through the years, but we are in touch often. Daddy's wife Charlotte and her family have been kind and caring, and for that I am very appreciative.

Buck and his father, Harry Glen Clark, Sr., pictured in 2006.

THE CLARK CLAN

Before moving on to my days at Berrien County High and in regard to Harry Clark and rest of the "Clark Clan," I'll take this opportunity to state that I am blessed to have two half siblings who are more like "buddies" than siblings. I know how special it is to be able to call siblings friends. Brother Mike Clark and his wife, Shaun, are always in touch, and we have a blast together. There is never a dull or negative moment with those guys. We love you.

Sister Mandy and her husband, Brad Shafer, are seasoned travelers with journeys as far as China. She is off-the-charts smart. Mandy reminds me so much of her late mother, Fritzie, because of her giving and caring spirit. Brad is kind and considerate; those two make a great team. Always a blast when the Clark Clan assembles– always a pleasure. Thanks guys.

The Clark Clan, pictured front, left to right, include Bob Bugbee, husband of my sister Diane, and sister Mandy, husband Brad Shafer. Pictured back row left to right are Buck, Jeanne, my sister-in-law, Shaun, and brother, Mike.

NEW NAME – NEW SCHOOL

Papa James had nicknamed me "Buck" back in the wing-backed chair days when I would jump, in his words, like a "wild buck" in my anticipation of getting a piece of Juicy Fruit gum. Although I was now officially named Mark Stephen, the name "Buck" stuck with me and remains to this day. So at the age of 14 in September, 1962, I entered a new school with a new name and new friends. It was the beginning of a new stage in my life.

I liked football from the start. I wanted to play quarterback and that was always my position. Having big hands, I could handle the ball and throw it pretty well. Speed was another issue.

Although I was optimistic, realistically the program was not very good. The school was county consolidated, and we lived on the extreme south end of Berrien County. Many kids like me lived a considerable distance from Nashville, and it made getting home after practice a major issue, especially for those of us who were under the driving age of 16.

Berrien County, which had a relatively low per capita income, was dominated by agriculture. Most kids in the county had to pitch in on the farm to help pay bills. Consequently, many parents refused to allow their kids to participate in sports and other after-school activities. I often thought we had a better team walking the halls of BHS than we did on the football field.

Regardless, I wanted to play, and Bee and Pop helped me every way they could. However, the sixteen-mile trip from Nashville to our farm was just too much for Pop to do every day. I had no choice but to hitchhike home on many occasions.

MY HITCHHIKING DAYS

Hitchhiking back then was not like it is now. I knew every farmer from Nashville to Barretts, and most of them knew my situation. Many times the same farmer would pick me up just outside of Nashville in his red pickup and take me as far as Charlie Mack's shop, where Pop would pick me up for the last two-mile leg.

Having to hitchhike home was tough after long practices, and sometimes the red truck was not available. Pop and I had a set time to meet at Charlie Mac's shop. If I was not there, he would backtrack to Nashville. There were times when it was well after dark, and I was eight miles or farther from home. On the day before games the coaches always found me a way home.

I was a starting quarterback for four years at Berrien County High, from the ninth grade junior varsity team through three years on the varsity squad.

The ninth grade JV season during the fall of 1962 was a period of learning. I think we won only one game. Although I played well and liked the sport, the ordeal of spending the day at school, going through football practice, and having to hitchhike home was tough.

As a fifteen-year-old in August of 1963 I began my first season on the varsity as backup to a senior quarterback. However, he broke his leg in practice before the first game, and the job of starting QB for the Berrien County High Rebels was mine for the next three years.

It was a struggle to compete with the deeper and much more talented teams in the Region 1-AA West, but we played as well as we could. We won only one or two games each season.

Because of our lack of size we threw the ball a great deal and had some success. Our defense, however, had issues, especially in stopping the Notre Dame Box offense of Fitzgerald and Ocilla.

A not so pleasant memory during my high school football career at Berrien County High occurred at Fitzgerald High School in the fall of 1964 when our coach forced us to do "Oklahoma Drills" outside the locker room during halftime in full view of all the fans. It was insane. Can you imagine going one-on-one outside the locker room during halftime with everybody watching? How embarrassing and humiliating was that! I lost all respect for our coach after that spectacle. He was replaced at the end of the season.

We gave it all we had, but the level of our talent simply did not compare with the majority of our opponents.

From the very beginning at BHS, I wanted to play basketball. But there was just no way to make it home every night after practice, especially as the days got shorter and most of the trip home was at night. Although I somehow managed to play baseball and run track during my freshman and sophomore years, transportation continued to be a problem.

I was a three-year starter for the Berrien County High Rebels from 1964 to 1966.

When I was thirteen, Pop co-signed a note at the Citizens Bank to buy me a mower. On summer Saturday mornings we loaded my trusty Briggs and Stratton 22" push mower into Pop's truck before daylight, and he unloaded me at Nanny's house on the corner of town. Saving my money from working on the farm and from mowing what seemed like every yard in Ray City, I began making payments on the mower when I was thirteen and paid it off in two summers.

Pop always made me check the oil. It seemed as if he was more concerned about the oil than the gas. He would often say, "Run all day without gas if you want to, but do not ever run the mower without oil."

On my sixteenth birthday in 1964, my transportation problems dramatically changed when Pop asked me to join him outside the house for a minute. I walked out the door and saw a beautiful 1958 green, four-door Studebaker parked under the pecan tree. Pop always said if a car only had two doors he wanted them both on the same side. Pop made the selection, and I was off the charts! My car could have been a Rolls Royce, and I would not have been any more excited. The arrangement with Pop was for me to pay half from my grass-cutting earnings, and he would pay half. We would split the insurance cost. Pop wrote a check out of my custodial account, and he matched it. We paid cash, and my hitch-hiking days were history! Needless to say, Pop gave me the "oil speech" time and again. For at least a year after getting the car I checked the oil every day.

COACH STANLEY "RAMROD" SIMPSON

At the end of my sophomore year and with my transportation problems solved, I called Coach Stanley "Ramrod" Simpson, the BHS head basketball coach, and asked him if I could try out for basketball after the upcoming football season ended. He agreed. I could now compete in all sports at Berrien County High.

Coach Simpson was an awesome person who was devoted to his team. I think he had some issues with the way some of the football players had been mistreated. Motivating and coaching his players from a positive perspective, Coach Simpson knew the game and built confidence in us. He was a brilliant game coach under pressure and literally out-coached many opponents with the use of time outs, backcourt traps, and full-court pressure.

On one occasion we were playing Cairo, our arch rival in Region 1-AA West, on our home court. Cairo was the region favorite, but we were a close second. We started the game cold and could not make a shot from anywhere. We were down by 14 points at the mid way mark of the first quarter.

After I missed five consecutive shots, Coach Simpson took me out of the game and gave me a dose face-to-face with teeth snarled. He actually spit in my face, unintentionally. He expected only the best.

The refs immediately slapped Coach Simpson with a technical foul. Following some vigorous discussion with the zebras, he was ejected from the game.

Coach Simpson signaled the referee and called time out. Fuming but under control, he calmly walked over to team manager, Milton "Tank" Sizemore, and asked him to hand him the wide broom used to sweep the floor.

Tank looked at Coach and said incredulously, "What?"

Coach confirmed his request with a more convincing tone, and Tank gave him the broom. He took the broom, walked out on to the court, and turned it upside down. He then inserted the handle into the bottom of the home basket and rotated it around as if the basket was covered with an invisible cover.

The refs immediately slapped Coach Simpson with a technical foul. Following some vigorous discussion with the zebras, he was ejected from the game. Cairo made the two free throws from the technical, but we caught fire, shot 70 percent from the floor during the remainder of the game, and won in a close finish as "Ramrod" watched from his office adjacent to the court. Only Coach Simpson could have pulled something like that off!

Although he could have coached at a much higher level if he had chosen, Coach Simpson loved Berrien County. We won several region championships and consistently had winning seasons under his watch. Coach Simpson and I became very close as our relationship developed into my senior year.

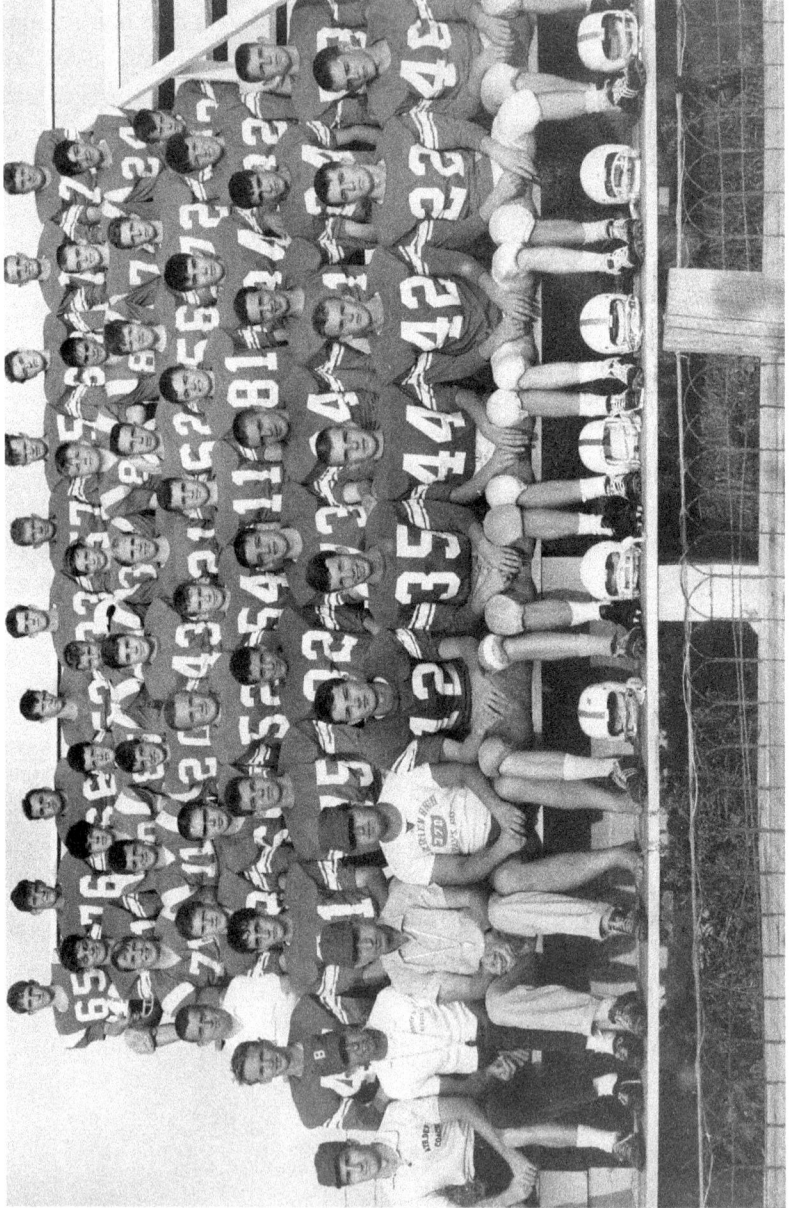

The 1966 Berrien County High School Rebel Football team. Seated second from left on the front row is Coach Stanley "Ramrod" Simpson. I am seated fifth from the left wearing #12.

MY FIRST SIGNIFICANT AWARD

One of the most prestigious awards in our area was called the "Tift Area Athlete of The Year Award," a citation that recognized overall excellence in athletics, academics, leadership and commitment. Athletes at several schools from all classifications in the large geographic area were eligible for consideration

Near the end of my senior year in 1966 I was selected as the nominee for the "Tift Area Athlete of The Year Award" from Berrien County High. Coach Simpson was our athletics director, and I think it was his idea to nominate me. Although I was honored to represent BCHS, I did not think I had a chance against kids from programs like Fitzgerald, Ocilla, Tifton, Lowndes, Brooks County, Ashburn, Cordele, and other surrounding schools.

But I was wrong. The area selection committee chose me as the 1966 recipient, and I was blown away. It was the first really significant award that I had ever won.

Coach Simpson, Bee, Pop, and I made the trip to Tifton for the presentation. All of the nominees attended the presentation, and several of them already had major college athletic scholarship offers. One of my fellow nominees was Hugh Gordon of Tifton High School. Hugh and I would later become teammates at the University of Georgia.

It was a great night as Coach Simpson had some special things to say about me. I made some brief remarks between cracks in my voice. It was uncharted waters for me, but the experience and association with those guys that night really helped my confidence in years to come.

Later that night, Coach Simpson, who never had children with his wife, Miss Betty Jo, paid me one of the most cherished compliments anyone has ever bestowed on me. He spoke to Bee and Papa James in the hallway at the ceremony and told them that if he ever had the opportunity to have a son he would want him to be just like me. I am not sure I deserved a compliment of that magnitude, but it was an honor that I will always remember.

I stayed in touch with Coach Simpson during my years at Riverside Military Academy and UGA. He always told me that I had the talent to play at a Southeastern Conference school. "Ramrod"--- we never called him that to his face--- is no longer with us, but I will never forget him. He was a great friend and confidant, and what he did for me will always be appreciated.

THE BLANK DIPLOMA

Winning the "Tift Area Athlete of the Year Award" was one of the highlights of my young life. However, another event around the same time is not something that I remember with pride. It was an experience of "guilt by association," but I suffered the consequences just the same.

During my last week of high school at BHS, some "friends" asked me to go to the school and "decorate" some of the trash cans, supposedly with some erasable chalk that was harmless. I did not want to be a snob or pooper so I jumped in. We waited until midnight, and I was asked to drive. The chalk turned out to be spray paint. When I saw what was going on I immediately flashed the lights to go.

The following morning the Berrien County Deputy Sheriff presented Papa James with a warrant for my arrest on the front steps of our farmhouse in full view of neighbors. Following extensive interrogation, personal apologies, and agreement to community service and financial restitution, the administrators allowed us to walk at the graduation ceremony. However, we would not receive diplomas. The graduation folders were the same as everyone, but the inside was blank. The incident was kept quiet. I was embarrassed for me and for my family. This could not be the same guy who only a few weeks before had won the Tift area award for community involvement and academic-athletic excellence, could it?

After performing our required community service work during the summer we privately received our official diplomas. What a dumb screw-up! I knew those guys were trouble, but I could not say no. I would have never pulled a stunt like that on my own! I just got caught up in the moment and wanted to be accepted. To this day I am embarrassed to tell this story.

III

PAPA JAMES AND BEE

Before sharing memories of the next stage of life following
graduation from Berrien County High School and leaving
home, I want to take this opportunity to share one of the things
of which I am most proud: my relationship with my parents.

My father, James Swindle, who I called "Papa James" and "Pop," and
my mother, Betty Swindle, who was and is still called "Bee," have always
been two of the most important people in my life.

Pop was a decorated World War II hero and bomber pilot who was extremely dedicated to his country and to his work. He was a born farmer and patriot and was a very committed person from a religious standpoint, especially in his later years. I give my mother credit for that conversion.

He was also a great athlete. Had it not been for WWII, it is very likely he would have played in the major leagues as a center fielder or third baseman.

During the years that we were together, Pop and I were more like best friends than we were father and son. He entered God's Kingdom of Heaven on September 10, 1993, and I miss him every day.

My mother, Bee, has always been the conduit of our family in every respect. She believed in doing everything that she could to make life as good as possible for Diane and me when we were growing up. She believed in commitment and hard work, and when school was over it was time to go to work. She also expected us to sustain ourselves once we had completed our education.

Bee remains today a tremendously devout Christian and a very strong person in terms of her character, her commitment to her church, and her ability to interact and communicate with people in a very positive way.

To follow are some of my fondest memories of these two wonderful people.

PAPA JAMES

The most important man in my life, Papa James, was born James A. Swindle on January 1, 1920. He was delivered by a midwife in the house where he lived for most of his adult life in Ray City, Ga. Ray City is located in the middle of Berrien County in southern Georgia.

Papa James was nine years old when the Great Depression hit, and he often spoke about its effects. He said that times were tough during that period, but "folks like us were used to hard times, and it was not nearly as serious for rural folk compared to the city folk." Pop said that farm people grew what they ate and never really had any money to speak of. "The billionaires who were in the breadlines were the real victims," he said. "We were already hard-nosed and equipped to stand hard times."

Having worked in his father Big Daddy's cotton gin growing up, Papa James said that many of the cotton farmers could not pay for gin fees in the late 20s and early 30s. However, Big Daddy would not take their cotton as collateral because he knew they needed the cotton to feed their families. Big Daddy never got paid in many cases. I can relate. (But more about that later.)

Papa James remembered that the bootleg business was huge back in those days because of Prohibition. He knew many local "shine farmers" growing up. Most of the locals sympathized with the "shine boys," but I think the "Revenuers" had a different view.

Pop stayed on the go on the farm day and night. Born and bred a dedicated farmer from his earliest remembrance, Papa James loved the outdoors and was the best dove shot on the planet. I sat with Pop on many dove shoots and noticed how other hunters would speak kindly to him and then move to the other side of the field. Pop shot a 20 gauge model 12 Remington at everything that flew. That shotgun remains one of my treasured possessions. There is even more history concerning this shotgun that I will relate later in this section as part of my thoughts on my mother, Bee.

Deadly on a dove field and very fond of duck hunting, Papa James could also walk you in the ground quail hunting. He is the only hunter I have ever known who bagged the limit on doves, ducks and quail in the same day. I had the feathers and guts to prove it.

Pop was also a steadfast conservationist. He would set wire quail traps, capture the birds, and then relocate them to sites on the farm where few birds had been seen. He never owned a mounted animal. He hunted for food, fun, and conservation.

Papa James fished as a boy and could literally smell out the bream beds with the best of them. He always said smell is the most important part of fishing. I do not believe he owned a bass rig. He called a bass a trout and so did everybody else. Papa James was a bream man, and he liked it when Preacher Shaw and I came in with a fresh mess. We called Sweet to do the cooking.

Known throughout south Georgia as a great athlete, Papa James played all sports at Ray City High School and received a multi-sport athletic scholarship to South Georgia College in Douglas, Ga. His best sport was baseball, and after the war he played in several professional organizations, including Jacksonville Terminal in what then was then AA minor league. He always said he thought he was good enough to play in the majors had it not been for World War II. It took four years out of what would have been his prime. But he never regretted serving his country and how well he did!

FLYING THE B-26 BOMBER IN WORLD WAR II

Pop was 21 years old on December 7, 1941 when his family gathered around the radio and listened to President Roosevelt's famous "Day of Infamy" speech to a joint session of Congress. He had been keeping up for some time with what had been going on in Europe with the advancement of Nazi tyranny, but few people, according to Pop, were concerned about the Japanese. He later said that our leadership had grossly underestimated the fury of the Japanese. He did not want any part of the Pacific Theatre.

I remember him saying, "Our country has to fight two global fronts at the same time without the resources to fight one. Never before has our country been faced with such a monumental task."

Papa James was a hardcore south Georgia farm boy. He knew about 100 degree "sand lugs croppin' days," plowing a mule from daylight to dark, fixing whatever was broken, treating any animal that needed care, and operating virtually any piece of farm equipment with precision. His farm experience proved to be invaluable as he faced the challenge of a lifetime.

> I remember him saying, "Our country has to fight two global fronts at the same time without the resources to fight one. Never before has our country been faced with such a monumental task."

Pop had a quick decision to make. Europe or the Pacific? His decision took five seconds. It would be Europe.

But what area of combat— infantry or air? He chose the Army Air Force. He considered all the aircraft in the American arsenal and chose the B-26 Martin Marauder.

Pop did not know at the time of his decision that the B-26 would later be nicknamed "The Widow Maker" and "The Flying Coffin." During his initial training at Tampa Bay the slogan, "one a day in Tampa Bay," was coined due to high loss of life and aircraft. The B-26 was like flying a heavyweight fighter. It was slow to take off, but hot to land and was designed to land on short runways.

Although many pilots wanted to fly the long range B-17 Flying Fortresses, there was a huge need for pilots to fly medium range bombers like the B-26. The B-26's were designed for location in England and flown across the English Channel to hit targets in occupied France and other western European countries occupied by the Nazis.

During World War II, Papa James flew a B-26 Marauder, as pictured above.

The B-26 entered service with the 8th Air Force in England in early 1943 with the 322nd Bomb Group, flying its first missions in May 1943. On the second mission across the Channel, an unescorted attack on a power station at Ijmuiden, Netherlands, the entire attacking force of 10 B-26s was lost to anti-aircraft fire and nearly 200 Luftwaffe fighters. Following this disaster the UK-based B-26 force was switched to medium altitude operations and transferred to the 9th Air Force where it was to support the planned invasion of France a year later in June, 1944.

At one point the B-26 was almost scrapped. But many modifications were made, and the aircraft later became very dependable and a tremendous asset in regaining control of France and the other occupied countries.

Papa James told me that he loved the escort fighters, but for most of the war there was not a fighter that had the range to take them all the way to the target and back until the P-51 Mustang came on the scene in January, 1944. With the new Mustang leading the way he said that he quickly knew it was just a matter of time before they would be kicking the German Luftwaffe's butts. Papa James was right as the Mustang quickly racked up huge kill ratios while protecting American bombers and greatly eclipsing the efforts of the P-47 Thunderbolt that had been previously used as escort fighters.

Papa James told me that he believed the advent and effectiveness of the P-51 Mustang significantly shortened the war in Europe. Once again, he was right. As noted in a 2010 documentary produced by The History Channel, "World War II in HD," the Mustang was credited as being a major factor in crippling the German air force which allowed the Allies to take control of the skies over Europe and pave the way for the successful D-Day invasion in June, 1944.

By the time Pearl Harbor was attacked by the Japanese in December, 1941, Germany had already occupied France, Belgium, and all the lower countries. I can remember sitting on the front porch at Rolling Green Farm and Pop telling me it was by the Grace of God that Hitler was not successful in conquering Great Britain and that most Americans had no idea just how many American pilots were fighting with the Royal Air Force in the Battle of Britain.

He also said, "Can you imagine such a military genius as Hitler deciding not to invade England by sea and directing his efforts to conquer Russia? That decision or non-decision was from God's hand and was the key to the fall of the Third Reich."

Pop really admired Winston Churchill when he made his famous statement, "Never in the face of human conflict has so much been owed by so many to so few."

I can remember him saying, "You want to talk about faith. The Brits had to have faith when they were being bombed every night and could not even strike a match!"

He reminded me of the famous British rescue at Dunkirk prior to the American involvement in the war. The British people assembled john boats, small fishing boats, pontoons, or anything that could enter the shallow waters of that section of northern France to rescue the valiant British infantrymen from certain death at the hands of the Nazis. It was one amazing story of bravery and honor.

Papa James spoke very little about his participation in the war, but he did share with me the time when a Messerschmitt fighter had him at point blank range. He could actually see the whites of the German fighter pilot's eyes as he approached from twelve o'clock. His nose gunner was out of 50 cals, and it was not good. But for some reason the fighter did not fire. Pop has no idea why he was not killed instantly by that fighter except that God had a different idea.

He also shared with me his experience of having golf ball size anti-aircraft flak penetrating the fuselage of his plane and narrowly missing his left leg. I have a piece of that flak today.

Then there was the evening prior to a mission when he said good night to the pilots occupying cots on either side of him. The following night both cots were empty.

When the B-26 crews returned from missions they gathered at the Swan Inn in Bury St. Edmunds, Suffolk, England to refresh and carve their names into the bar.

Papa James flew 56 of his 74 combat missions prior to the D-Day invasion on June 6th, 1944. All of those missions were flown across the English Channel and into occupied France and Belgium. Most of the targets were oil fields, transportation depots and military arsenals. One of the primary target zones was near a town in France called Beau Telle.

A typical mission was five to six hours in length with no heat. Temperatures were often near or below freezing for the entire duration of

Papa James (kneeling far right) with his B-26 crew of the *Sarah E.*

the flight! The weather over the English Channel was often treacherous and unpredictable. Pop insisted more planes were lost due to weather than from Nazi flack or Luftwaffe attacks. He often mentioned a phenomenon called "Purple Haze," a dense fog of extreme proportions that made it even difficult to read instruments inside the fuselage.

Ironically, Pop flew his last 18 missions from an airfield established by the 82nd Airborne liberators near the village of Beau Telle, France, yes one his former targets. Papa James's plane, the Sarah E, was awarded one of the most coveted military aviation awards in the war. The two 750 hp, Pratt-Whitney engines mounted on the wings of the Sarah E flew more hours of operation than any other B-26 during the entire European Theatre of Operations. Pop was quick to give the credit to the quality of service afforded by the ground crew, but the precision of the operating crew of the aircraft was a key factor as well.

I have Papa James's original log book. It is a family treasure. He "signed up" for only 25 missions but made 74 before he came home. His accomplishment is even more extraordinary when considering a fact noted in the recent History Channel special. A total of 75 percent of the entire 8th Air Force bomber crewmen never reached the 25th mission milestone. There is no doubt that Papa James was fortunate, especially considering the number of missions that he flew. When the 8th Air Force was created in Savannah, Georgia, a month after the attack on Pearl Harbor, there was a total of eight pilots and zero planes. By the time the war in Europe ended, more than three and one-half years later more than 26,000 airmen of the 8th Air Force had been killed.

Pop named his plane the Sarah E after his mother, Sarah Daniel Swindle. Flying other planes occasionally if the Sarah E needed repair, he flew the Sarah E on most of his 74 combat missions.

According to Papa James, the ground crew "made the mission." He also said that he had the best ground crew in the bomb group. I suppose he was right because the Sarah E's engines, two 750 HP Pratt-Whitneys, flew more successful combat missions and total hours than any other B-26 in the European Theatre of Operations.

Pop was always quick to say that he did not fly all of the Sarah E's missions due to the fact that the plane remained in service after his last mission, but he flew most of them. The Sarah E was finally shot down in action in 1945 after Pop had completed his combat tour.

Papa James piloted 74 combat missions over Europe during World War II.

PAPA JAMES' WAR RECORD

On the following pages is a chronological account of Papa James's war record in my mother's handwriting and reproduced in its original form. It's a treasure.

James A. Swindle:

Was first cadet ever sworn in at Turner Field, Albany, Ga. — Jan. 3, 1942. The next day was given a train ticket to Maxwell Field, Montgomery, Ala. After getting uniforms, transferred to Dothan, Ala. for approximately three weeks. After about a month was transferred back to Maxwell. From there to Flying School (Primary) - at Lodwick Air Force Academy, Avon Park, Fla. First flight there was on Feb. 25, 1942 in PT-17. Graduated April 24, 1942 with 60 hours and 8 minutes of flying time. From there to Greenville, Miss. on May 3, 1942, flying BT-13A. Graduated July 1, 1942 with 71 hours and 45 minutes of flying time in BT-13A's. From there to Columbus, Miss. on July 10th, 1942, flying

AT-17's and AT-9's, graduating Sept. 6, 1942 after 71 hours and 30 minutes, in Advance there, receiving Wings and Commission as 2nd. Lt. Total flying time in Flying School was 203 hours and 25 minutes, and 28 hours and 40 minutes in link trainer. Reported to MacDill Field, Tampa, Fla. Sept. 15, 1942. B-26's were grounded when he arrived at MacDill due to loss of 18 crashes in 18 days at Mac Dill. The phrase — "a ship a day in Tampa Bay" — was coined from that incident. Took his first ride in a B-26B Oct. 8, 1942. Was assigned to 451st. Bomb Squadron of the 322 nd. Bomb Group. Nov. 20th. moved to Drane Field in Lakeland, Fla. and lived under simulated combat conditions. On Feb. 9, 1943, moved to Warner Robins Air Force Base, Macon, Ga., to bullet-proof our gas tanks, in preparation for going overseas. We returned to MacDill March 5, 1943. April 10, 1943 concluded flying at MacDill, with a total flying time of 346 hours and 35 minutes, and 37 hours and 40 minutes in link trainer. On April 14, 1943, we started overseas, going to Morrison Field, West Palm Beach, Fla. April 16, 1943 - Morrison Field to Boringuen, Puerto Rica. April 18 - " " to Waller Field, Trinidad.

April 20th - From Waller Field to Atkinson Field, British Guiana, South America.
April 21st - to Belem, Brazil, " "
" 25th " Natal, " " "
" 29th " Ascension Island, So. Atlantic Ocean
" 30th " Roberts Air Base, Liberia, Africa.
May 1st " Dakar, French West Africa
" 3rd " Tindouf, French Morocco, Africa
" 7th " Marrakech " " "
" 12th " Port Lyautey " " "
" 14th " Talbenny, Wales, British Isles
" 15th " St. Eval in England
" 15th " Rattlesden " "

Flying time on trip overseas was 69 hours and 20 minutes. On June 7th to Prestwick, Scotland to ferry an airplane back to Wharton, England. June 7th - from Wharton to Snetterton Heath, England. June 12th - from Bury St. Edmunds to Great Balling, Braintree, England. May 17th two squadrons out of our group, the 322nd. Bomb Group, 8th Air Force, sent 10 airplanes on a mission to Ijmuiden, Holland, with none returning. They went in at low level, according to our training at O altitude. B-26's were grounded, as a result of 10 for 10 losses, and we started training at 12,000 feet. We were put back in Operations, going on my first mission July 28, 1943 at 12,000 feet, on a diversionary raid in France. Oct. 16, 1943 we transferred to the Ninth Air force. I named my airplane "Sarah E", after my Mother, remembering that she had never let me down. This "Sarah E" did likewise. After flying 61 missions over Belgium, France. and Holland, I was allowed to come home for 30 days. Left Liverpool, England, approximately May 20th. 1944, on the Mauretania, arriving in New York Harbor. After 30 days at home, back to Atlantic City, awaiting orders to go back overseas. Return trip was also on the Mauretania, leaving from Boston Harbor. Back to England on August 4, 1944. Back to combat on Aug. 9th, after flying five days of local practice bombing. Sept. 29th. 1944, we moved from Andrews Field, England to Beauvais Tille, France, a field we had bombed many times from England. On Nov. 9, 1944 I made my 74th.

and final mission, leading a box, consisting of 18 airplanes, to Stuttgart, Germany. This gave me a total of 803 hours and 45 minutes flying time, 47 hours and 40 minutes in link trainers and 197,800 pounds of bombs dropped in France, Belgium, Holland and Germany.

Left France for England approximately Nov. 15, 1944. Left Liverpool approximately Dec. 19, on New Amsterdam, arriving in Halifax, Nova Scotia on Christmas Day, 1944. From there to Miami Beach and was assigned to the Don Cassar Hotel in St. Petersburg, Fla. for rest and reassignment.

Approx. April 10, 1945 to Laughlin Field, Del Rio, Texas. May 1st. to Bryan Field, Bryan, Texas, for Instrument Training. On June 10th. final flight at Bryan Field, giving me a total of 903 hours and 55 minutes flying time.

Graduated Sep. 6, 1942 as a 2nd Lt.
10 months later promoted to 1st. Lt. (1943)
8 " " " " Captain (1944)

Awards in E.T.O.

Aug. 31, 1943 — Air Medal
Sep. 8, " — Oak Leaf Cluster to Air Medal
Nov. 3, " — Second Oak Leaf Cluster - Bronze
Dec. 5, " — Third " " " "
Dec. 22, " — Distinguished Flying Cross
Feb. 3, 1944 - Fourth Oak Leaf Cluster - Bronze
Feb. 13, " — Fifth " " " — Silver
Feb. 29, " — Sixth " " " — Bronze
Mar. 5, " — Seventh " " " "
Mar. 17, " — Eighth " " " "
May 7, " — Ninth " " " "
May 15, " — Tenth " " " Silver
Aug 25, " — Eleventh " " " Bronze
Oct 9, " — Twelfth " " " "
Approx. May 15, 1943 - Caribbean Theater Medal
" Aug 15, " - The African - European
End of the war - Theater Medal
Good Conduct Medal
Presidential Group Citation

Approx. June 12, 1945, orders to go to Ft. McPherson in Atlanta for honorable discharge. Received discharge Aug. 5th, with 30-day leave. Discharged Sep. 5th, 1945, which was three years to the day as a Commissioned Officer.

Our Group had 150% losses

Dedication of a Squadron Memorial, at the Air Force Museum, Wright-Patterson Air Force Base, Dayton, Ohio, took place 17 July 1985. A tree was planted and an easel and bronze plaque placed beside it. 17 July was selected for the dedication date because, according to official Air Force records, that was the date that the Squadron was activated in 1942 and flew its first combat sortie in 1943. The dedication ceremony was held outdoors and at the conclusion a two-ship formation of USAF F-4 aircraft flew over while "Taps" was being played by a Bugler from the Air Force Band. The plaque has the Squadron logo in the upper left corner and a raised B-26 in the upper right corner. The inscription on the plaque is as follows:

In Honor of
The Men Who Served the
451 ST. Bombardment Squadron
322 nd. Bombardment Group (M)
Flew 301 Combat Missions in
B-26 Marauders
From England, France and Belgium
During World War II
6 Campaigns in European Theater
of Operations
Distinguished Unit Citation:
ETO, 17 July 1943 – 24 July 1944
"Our Fallen Comrades Are Not Forgotten"
Activated: MacDill Field, Fla – 17 July 1942
Inactivated: Camp Kilmer, New Jersey – 11 Dec 1945
Dedicated – 17 July 1985

BACK TO THE FARM

When Papa James returned from the war it was back to the farm. He was a war hero, and everyone in Ray City and the surrounding area was proud of him, as well they should have been. He was very fortunate to have survived and made such a valuable contribution.

Pop always had the faith. He was an eternal optimist and never looked at the glass as half empty. Returning from the war, he buckled down and went to work on his own to make a go of the farm.

Papa James was a gentleman, a great caregiver, a compassionate man, a rugged individualist, a man of courage, a man of few words, and a man of purpose. He was a political conservative, and Barry Goldwater was his hero. He later admired Ronald Reagan and considered him the greatest president in American history. I think I know what his views on today's political environment would be. He probably has a "tea party" going on somewhere.

Papa James stressed the importance of integrity, and I never once saw him compromise that integrity. At one time, Pop and I were business partners. He loved his cattle, and during my years with Warren Sewell Clothing Company and up until his passing, we owned a beautiful herd of registered Brahman and Simmental cattle. Those were great years we shared together. We traveled to shows and meetings and just hung out together. I cannot say the cattle business was a huge profit center, but the experiences that we shared made it a gold mine to us both.

Simply stated, Papa James was the best friend I ever had. We were inseparable and did everything together. On the farm we were working partners and shared a great respect for each other.

On September 10, 1993, Papa James joined an elite group in the company of God's Heaven. His life celebration was beautiful. Music Funeral Home did a very good job, and Biff Coker, pastor of Valdosta First Presbyterian, did a great job with the service, as did the late Jim Callahan, former Rector at St. Margaret's Episcopal Church in Carrollton. A special thanks goes to Biff and Jim.

I do have one regret regarding Papa James's service, and that is I should have been involved and had my say. I have gone over my comments a thousand times since.

I imagine there is a beautiful, lush field of arrow leaf clover up there where a white GMC truck is parked with the tail gate down. I can see Papa James hand feeding range cubes to his heifers. I speak to Papa James every day.

Papa James enjoying his pride and passion.

Pictured above are "Doddy" (standing right) and his grandchildren. Standing are Paula Patten and Lee Roquemore Burton. Kneeling are Bob Roquemore (left) and Jim Roquemore. Sitting on the couch left to right are Pat Roquemore, Rocky Roquemore, sister Diane, and Buck holding Baby Lawson Patten.

MY MOTHER, BEE

My mother, Betty Patten Swindle, will always be known as "Bee" to family and friends. She nicknamed herself, and it fits her well. Bee was born in Lakeland, Ga., May 6, 1922. Her parents were Lawson Leo Patten and Clyde Purcell Patten of Lakeland. Bee has quite a family.

As my Aunt Nell so truly stated in her introduction of my mother's father, "Doddy," my grandfather did what he wanted to, when he wanted to, and the way he wanted to. A truly dedicated public servant, he was chairman of the Lanier County Board of Education in 1924, was elected mayor of Lakeland in 1925, and was a member of the Georgia State Legislature from 1928 to 1936. He was appointed by Gov. Ed Rivers to the Georgia State Highway Board in 1939 and later was elected Chairman of the Board.

Doddy was an entrepreneur and loved agriculture. He had an idea in the fall of 1946 to sell Bermuda grass sprigs commercially. He later formed a seed cleaning business. From that beginning and with the leadership of my Uncle Bill Roquemore that followed, Patten Seed Company came into existence. The company today is more commonly known as Super Sod, one of the largest producers of turf grass and related products in the southeastern United States.

The Roquemores also developed the concept of affordable golf in the Atlanta area with the creation of the Canongate network of golf courses. I can remember the night at our home in Ray City when Aunt Nell and Bee got out the Encyclopedia Britannica in search for a name for the first golf course. I believe they came up with the name that evening at our home. Canongate— what a great name taken from a street in Edinburgh, Scotland where the game of golf originated.

AUTHOR'S NOTE

I want to thank Uncle Bill, Aunt Nell, my cousins Rocky, Jim, Pat, Bob, Lee and all their families for everything that they have done for our family over the years. A special thanks goes to the Rocks.

MY FIRST RECOLLECTION OF BEE

My birth name was Harry Glen Clark, Jr. Diane, my sister, was 17 months older. My first memory of Bee was when I was four years old. We lived in a "lavish" downtown apartment on North Ashley Street in Valdosta, Ga. Bee went through a divorce from my father, Harry Clark, and we moved from Thomasville to Valdosta where she began a new career in advertising with the local radio station. Valdosta was a good fit for Bee in that she could start her new career in a great town and be near her father, Doddy, who lived nearby in Lakeland.

The three of us were very close. Bee would read to Diane and me every night. Diane often bossed me around, but that was okay. She and I had, and have to this day a great relationship.

Bee insisted that Di and I help with chores. I suppose that is one trait I especially appreciated in Bee. She was a great giver of love and gifts, but she expected everyone to carry their load. Bee was very generous and compassionate, but she could spot it in a minute when she felt someone was taking advantage of her.

She also could be just as tough as she needed to be when the time came for dealing with family or whomever. She continues to have an extraordinary ability to "discern" people. She really did not like the term 'judge,' since she believed that was God's job, not hers. She liked the

Apostle Paul's approach when he preached to the Philippians and spoke of the importance of gaining knowledge as a prerequisite to making good decisions, something Bee calls "discernment."

I have always believed that God has placed angels on earth and commissioned them to influence others and be spiritual leaders. I believe that these mortal angels are rare in number, and you have to be on the constant lookout to find them. But when you make the connection it is powerful beyond description. I have been so fortunate to have one of those special mortal angels as my mother.

Faith is Bee's strength. I never, yes never, have experienced a time when she lost her composure or raised her voice. I realize that is difficult to believe, but it is the truth.

The same goes for profanity and arguments. Bee has such a strong commitment to Jesus Christ in her life. She has never given Christ's adversaries— fear, hate, sloth, judgment, anxiety, and all that negative stuff--- an opportunity to take over her life. It just ain't gonna happen with her.

Shortly after Bee and Papa James's marriage in February, 1954 we moved to the farm, and Bee accepted a job with the Civil Service Procurement Office at Moody Air Force Base in Valdosta. It was an excellent employment opportunity, and she worked her way up to a Level 12 position in the civil service ranks, a very high ranking for a female employee at that time. She served for 26 years in that capacity.

The benefits from Bee's employment at Moody saved our family from financial collapse since it coincided with the terrible drought that hit our region and drastically curtailed farm production. Her retirement benefits were immensely important during the period of Papa James' advanced illness many years later.

TOUGH TIMES ON THE FARM

Beginning with Bee and Papa James's marriage and our move to the farm it was a new life for us. As I noted in the first chapter of this book regarding my early years growing up on the farm, times were tough that first year in 1954. A terrible drought hit, and Big Daddy, Papa James's father, died, which brought on additional responsibilities associated with his business that Papa James had to handle. It was farm-time tough, but neither Pop nor Bee ever let us know just how tough times were.

Bee was the backbone of the family. She worked many 12-15 hour days.

Pictured, from left to right, in 1965 are Aunt Nell Roquemore, my grandfather, Mr. L.L. Patten; Bee; and her brother, Robert Patten.

She helped Diane and me get ready for school in the morning, got the job done at Moody, came home to cook and clean, and did whatever else needed doing. How she got it all done I still do not know. We all helped, but she carried the load.

Although we were members of the Ray City Baptist Church for many years and attended regularly, for some reason I never thought we quite fit in. Bee, although she had been a Presbyterian for many years, agreed to attend Ray City Baptist since it was the Swindle family tradition.

Bee was always the spiritual leader in the family, and she was and is today an avid reader of spiritual works. However, during those early years she did not have the time to read and grow spiritually as she would have liked due to her workload. She later became a teacher, leader, and speaker in all the churches and organizations in which she was involved.

Bee is a believer in constant "acquisition of knowledge" through the written word. She has read the Bible from cover to cover at least three times and has ministered to those in need at every church and community where she has been involved.

For me, however, church during those early years was like a chore and just another thing to do on the list.

One day Bee decided to make a change, and she did it all on her own. While Papa James continued to attend the Ray City Baptist Church, Bee decided to join the Valdosta First Presbyterian Church, USA. She soon became an inspirational leader, teacher and Elder under the direction of the church's great pastor, Dr. Biff Coker.

I believe when she made the decision to join VFPC that she really began to experience the Christian devotion that she had always desired. Shortly after Bee joined VFPC Papa James agreed to make the change. I believe at that point Papa James began a spiritual transformation. Bee and God did a double team on Papa James.

THE INTRUDER

Bee has a unique ability to remain calm in a crisis and be fearless. One event that sticks in my mind is a weeknight in 1962. It was about 10 p.m., and Papa James was at a cattlemen's meeting. Bee and I were at home alone relaxing and watching TV when I heard a loud voice coming from the middle of the highway in front of the house. It was someone screaming in a high pitched, profane voice. I looked out the window but I did not see anyone. I turned on the porch light, and there was still no sign of anyone.

I was 14 years old at the time and was very familiar with firearms. Bee and I walked around the house, and we continued to hear the loud, violent screaming. It was clearly someone who was deranged. Bee and I

Pop displays the fine doors and windows Uncle Razzee constructed on the house we lived in at Rolling Green Farm.

went to the center of the house and held hands and prayed for a minute. She then went to the closet and pulled out Pop's Model 12 20-gauge pump and said to me, "How do you use this?"

By this time, the screaming was louder and closer. Suddenly someone began kicking and hitting the outside of the front door and windows with his fists. I was terrified, but Bee was as calm as could be. I could not believe it.

Bee had no clue how to operate the pump, but I knew exactly how to use it. Pop and I had quail hunted and shot doves together since the move in '54, and I had used the pump many times. Pop always kept two shells in the magazine. It was button down and pump once to chamber a shell.

Telling me to sit down in front of our antique secretary just in front of the door, Bee calmly said, "Do not lot let that man hurt us."

After calling the sheriff, Bee sat me down in the floor with a shell in the barrel and the safety off. I watched the front door shake like a leaf every time he hit it. I just knew it would fly open any time. I had made up mind to shoot in the middle of the door if it opened.

I don't know how many times the man rammed the door. He went all the way around the house cursing and then returned to the front door for more attempts to break in. The attack lasted for 30 minutes from the first scream until the deputy sheriff roared in sideways off Highway 122, jumped out of his car, and chased the intruder down in the corn field behind our house.

Our house was 16 miles from the nearest large town, and it was unusual to see a Lowndes County deputy on what was the county line road. It just so happened that the deputy on patrol was within two miles of our house when Bee called.

As it turned out, the man had been "over-served" at a local liquor store-bar just to the east of our house. He told the authorities that he thought he was at his home. He lived about a mile down the road from us and was dropped off at the wrong house by a drinking buddy. He thought his wife was refusing to allow him to come in what he thought was his own house.

I often wonder if that man knew Uncle Razzee. He, as well as Bee and I, owe Uncle Razzee a huge thank you for the heavy duty door and hinges that he insisted we install when he remodeled the house eight years before.

The man later came back, brought food and apologized.

I grew up a bit that night, but more impressive was how Bee handled the situation: steadfast and under control. She has lived her life under control and with humility and purpose. Bee has always allowed God to lead her.

An extremely hard worker, she has applied herself in so many ways, but has never been obsessed with control or with material possessions. For her, it has always been about humility and patience.

BEE WAS FAST, BUT DIDN'T GET IN A HURRY

Bee had an earlier nickname and was known as Aunt Jennie. Our relative and close friend of Papa James, Jim Paulk, attached the moniker to Bee. The actual Aunt Jennie was an older relative who was known for moving at a slower than normal pace. I think of Coach John Wooden's famous quote, "You have to be fast, but you can't get in a hurry," applies so appropriately to Bee. She proceeds with life and her decisions with speed and accuracy, but does not physically rush to closure.

Never allowing herself to lose focus on her goals and objectives, Bee had no time for "bunko groups" or county club tennis-golf interests. She has always maintained simplicity in her life and has an incredible way of taking a seemingly complicated problem and developing a simple, direct solution.

I grew up working in the hay field and tobacco patch, playing ball, going to school and just having a great time. I was so fortunate to have an Angel for a mother. I think farm life makes you more aware of each other's needs, and you rely on siblings and other family members in a special way.

Bee supported me in all that I did, including my participation in athletics, school, work on the farm, and the decision to attend Riverside Military Academy in the fall of 1966. Bee cried when we left for RMA in Gainesville, Ga. that first day, but she knew it was right for me.

It was only a year later when Bee and I had a conversation from the Pi Kappa Alpha fraternity house in Athens concerning my treatment as a football player at UGA. All I needed from Bee was a hint of support for my decision to leave the program. But she avoided the emotion and focused on the solution. I often speculate how my life might have turned out if she had supported my desire to leave.

THE ST. SIMONS YEARS

In the early spring of 1991, I asked Bee and Pop why they did not get away more and enjoy places like St. Simons or Daytona. Although Pop was not interested since he just wanted to stay at home on the farm, Bee had an interest in venturing out.

My wife Jeanne and I spent several weekends at St. Simons, and we located a property at Sea Palms that seemed ideal for Papa James and Bee. We asked the realtor to hold one particular unit until we could get Bee and, hopefully, Pop to come and check it out.

It took two weeks, but we finally convinced them to take the time to visit St. Simons and relax some in the process. Once they saw the unit, it was all over. Bee closed on the property in the summer of 1991.

Bee and Pop enjoyed "Casabella," which was Bee's nickname for their new getaway. Pop loved it once he got there, but getting him there was the problem. Once he arrived he would chill out on one of the long sofas and really enjoyed it.

Bee moved permanently to "Casabella" shortly after Papa James's passing. It proved to be a great place for her to spend her "Golden Years." She loved everything about St. Simons and read every book that Eugenia Price ever wrote about that special place.

Thriving on grouper sandwiches at the Putters Club at Sea Palms, Bee joined the St. Simons Presbyterian Church, USA and became an instrumental session leader, teacher, and elder. A special thanks goes out to Rev. Bob Beirley and all the fine people at that great church who shared many good times with Bee at St. Simons.

Buck and Jeanne at "Weekend for Wildlife" at Sea Island in 2000.

Bee enjoyed many places and activities during her 13-year stay on St. Simons from the fall of 1993 until the spring of 2006. Specific memories of that period include the crab stew at Frederica House, crabbin' at the pier with those little guys and all the locals, my runs with her concerns to the traffic light on Frederica Road, the fishing trips to Two Way, the great seafood and camaraderie at Mudcat Charlie's, the walks down East Beach, the trolley rides, the trips to Christ Church and Ft. Frederica, the frequent trips to Harris Teeter, the rainy-day movies, and just the sheer beauty and tranquility of St. Simons Island--- an awesome gift of God's Creation.

Bee has a great love for St. Simons Island, Ga. and the St. Simons Presbyterian Church, USA where she served as a teacher, lay leader, elder, and member for 10 years.

BEE MAKES HER MOVE

On a spring day in 2006 I received a phone call from Bee. She immediately said hello and then talked for five minutes about how the time at St. Simons had been some of the most fulfilling years of her life.

But then Bee said that it was time for a change. She had selected a place near Jacksonville, Florida that she dearly loved and wanted to move immediately. She was determined and had her mind set— and that means business with Bee. Within two weeks of her call to me she was set up in her new home.

Bee is greatly blessed to be living a peaceful and fruitful life. At 89 years of age, she continues to be a wonderful loving, spiritual and giving lady.

MY SISTER, DIANE

As noted earlier in this chapter, Bee currently lives in Jacksonville, near my sister, Diane. I am so thankful for Diane and everything that she does for our mother, but also for so much more.

Diane is my great friend, advisor, and confidant. She has a special gift of giving and caring and looks for those in need as opposed to reacting to those coming to her in need. She has special gifts for learning and teaching and has more degrees than most schools offer.

An attorney by trade with the skills to make six figures with any law firm, Diane has chosen a different path. She performs many types of services for the abused women and children received by the Hubbard House in Jacksonville, Florida, a non-profit shelter for women in turmoil and transition. Her outreach goes well beyond the walls of the brick and mortar of that great facility. Diane's work is done tirelessly, and her income is secondary to her devotion to those with special needs and with little or no resources.

Thanks, Diane, for being such a great friend and the example you set as my big sister. Di is the deal!

One of the best things to happen to Aunt Di was meeting and marrying Bob Bugbee. When they married I was honored to be asked to lay read at the wedding. Bob has been an inspiration to our family, and he is the best husband I have ever known. All us guys should take "husband lessons" from Uncle Bobby.

We have become great friends, but you have to watch him on the trout-redfish trips to Egg Island out of Two Way when he captures the bow position as the grass line approaches. Aunt Di and Uncle Bobby provide the day-to-day support for Bee and for that I am grateful.

HEADS UP #3

Good parents make great friends

- Communicate every day, write in hand, and call.

- Laugh and play, and just have fun.

- Seek advice constantly. The best experience is often some else's. Yes, even your parents.

- Love 'em always.

- Make sure that the older your parents get the more you see them and the more you communicate with them.

- Sometimes you need space. Know your boundaries.

Honor your father and your mother, so that you may live long in the land of the Lord your God in giving you.

– Exodus 20:12

Ready for the Dress Parade at Riverside Military Academy in the fall of 1966.

After graduating from Berrien County High School in Nashville, Ga. in June of 1966, I had a decision to make. The thought of spending a postgraduate year between high school and college at Riverside Military Academy in Gainesville, Ga. had been on my mind for a while. Our family knew the school had an excellent reputation as a college prep institution, and my grandfather, Doddy, was a legacy.

Riverside was a member of the Mid-South Conference of prep schools at that time. The program, much like today's junior colleges, provided for a year of "grooming" prior to going to a major college Division I school. I was acquainted with several high school athletes who attended prep schools around the south, including Baylor, McCauley, Tennessee Military, Lowndes Academy, Castle Heights, and Riverside.

It was during my senior year at BHS that I decided I wanted to play football at the University of Georgia. At the time, a player from Berrien County High had never played on a SEC team or any Division I team. I had no idea how lofty that goal was at the time.

I decided that a year at Riverside Military Academy would allow me to grow and develop and maybe give me the experience I needed to play quarterback on the major college level. So on August 12, 1966, we loaded the car with trunks and duffle bags and headed to Gainesville, Ga. for fall football practice.

That day was memorable for two reasons: it was the first time I had ever been away from home for any length of time, and it was the first time that I had ever seen Papa James cry. We had been inseparable from the day we met in 1952 until that afternoon 14 years later.

It was a difficult day. Once we arrived, the school personnel did not allow me to dwell on the emotions of the moment. With duffle bag in hand and dragging my trunk up to the second floor of the Bravo Company dorm, I checked into my room. The room looked like a prison cell to me at first, but I later got used to it. I really liked its simplicity that included a double bunk, two desks, two chairs, and a tiny closet and adjoining bath.

By the time we said our goodbyes and Papa James and Bee were on the Hall County line, I had been given a buzz cut and was issued fatigues and football gear.

Within the next hour I met all the other cadet-football guys and the coaches. I met Coach McGinnis, our head coach, prior to the start of fall practice. I later met Coach Bisso, who was the assistant line and defensive coach.

A friend of mine from high school, Bob Gaskins, had agreed to come to RMA as my roommate when the fall term began. Bob played football in high school but elected not to play at RMA.

THE 1966 FOOTBALL SEASON
AT RIVERSIDE MILITARY ACADEMY

For the next three weeks all 45 players and coaches started putting together the 1966 Riverside Military Academy football team. The difficult task for a school like RMA is that it had no scholarships and never really knew who was coming back to school from year to year. The enrollment was comprised of young men from 35 states and approximately 20 percent were international students. However, many of the other Mid-South Conference schools had "ways" to be able to recruit certain top players who later went on to some of the major Division I schools.

During fall practice we noticed many local kids liked to ride by our practice and heckle us with chants of "River Rats Suck" and some other terms that I will not list. They really did not like us. I suppose we were considered different and not normal to them.

The dislike for cadets was even more evident at the Florida campus of Riverside Military Academy. RMA was a unique school at that time in that two completely different campuses were maintained. All cadets reported to Gainesville, Georgia to begin the fall term where we played the entire football season and half of the basketball season. Before we returned home for Christmas we were issued a plane ticket to Miami, Fl. In January we flew to Miami and attended the Ft. Lauderdale campus of

Riverside Military Academy until the spring break.

We played the last half of our basketball season in Florida and the first half of our baseball season as well. We traveled by bus from Florida back to Gainesville during spring break to complete the year.

The concept of two campuses was the dream and reality of the founder of RMA, General Sandy Beaver. The dual system was later terminated when the property in Florida was sold in the mid '70s.

My roommate and I were both assigned to Bravo Company where we had all the responsibilities as the non-football players. But I do believe that I did get one bit of preferential treatment regarding the M1 carbine. Every cadet had to be able to successfully clean an M1 semi-automatic shoulder weapon in 60 seconds. That included disassembling, cleaning and re-assembling in that short time frame. I always seemed to have two or three parts left over. It was just not my thing.

However, I think there was someone who thought I was making a contribution on the football field, because one day the company commander asked me if I wanted to be the Company "Guide On." He needed someone tall who could swing the tall company banner with authority. I did not know at the time how coveted that position was. One of the fringe benefits of serving as the Company Guide-On was not being required to clean the M1.

Since I was a three-year starter at quarterback at Berrien County High School I had every reason to believe that I would start at QB at Riverside. There was only one problem with that idea, and his name was David Fair. David was 6'2", 195 lb., ran a 4.6-40, had an arm like a rocket, was consensus All-State in Tennessee, and was a top recruit for the University of Tennessee. It took me about five minutes to discover that I needed to find another position on offense if I wanted to start.

I backed up Fair at quarterback and started at wide receiver on offensive and free safety on defense. David threw me nine TD's that year, and we both made the All-Mid South Offensive Team.

During the football season at Riverside in the fall of 1966, we played some top teams and lost only two games. We had five players from that team go on to play at the collegiate level. Fair went on scholarship to Tennessee Tech and played immediately. I walked on at the University of Georgia.

BASKETBALL MELEE AT RABUN GAP NACOOCHEE

Football was over now, and I had letters coming in from several colleges that expressed interest in me for the 1967 season. However, I learned quickly that there is a big difference between a letter of interest and a scholarship offer

In the meantime, with the football season completed, I really wanted to play basketball and did so immediately following the final football game. Colonel Nichols was our basketball coach and he was a good one. The guys who had played football were not in shape to run the court at first, but after a little work and sweat, it all came together. At 6'3", 180 pounds, I played center and forward.

RMA played primarily local schools since our seasons were split between the campus locations in Georgia and Florida. Rabun Gap-Nacoochee School at Rabun Gap in the northeast Georgia mountains was one of our top rivals. They hated the "River Rats," and we did not have a great deal of respect for those "mountain boys" either.

Rabun Gap-Nacoochee School, which played basketball year round was tucked away in a secluded part of the Georgia mountains about 90 minutes from Gainesville. The curvy roads into the mountains of north Georgia were certainly not what I had been accustomed to growing up in south Georgia. About an hour and a half into the trip I became queasy from the smell of diesel fumes and the winding roads.

Since I had never been to RGNS before, I was a little surprised to be greeted by the boo-birds who were out in full force. The gym was like a matchbox. It was probably 80 percent of regulation size, and it must have been 100 degrees inside. The sidelines could not have been more than three-feet from the first row of bleachers.

Although the gym was largely packed with RGNS locals, we did have a bus load of mandatory cadet attendants from Riverside present. Our fellow cadets proved to be a big help in our exit later in the evening.

RGNS played a straight man-to-man defense and pressed all night. I had a guy on me who reminded me of Lurch from "The Adam's Family." He looked to be eight feet tall and had elbows like razor blades. The officials could have just as well have been at the movies. It was more like a pick-up game than regulation.

Lurch was out to get me that night, and it got worse as the game progressed. I cannot recollect which team was ahead at the time, but I do remember that the ball was out on them, and I was attempting to make an inbounds play from the out of bounds in the middle of the court. Lurch was literally in my face and gave me no room to look for a teammate on the inbounds play. Someone sitting on the first row of the stands behind me was tugging on my shorts. I lost it!

I remembered that when in that position and with time running out you are supposed to bounce the ball off the opponent in order to get another five seconds to inbound. I did that, but... I used Lurch's nose as a target to bounce the ball out of bounds. It was like a 70-foot Georgia pine hitting the ground during a clear-cut. There was blood everywhere.

Both benches emptied. The large contingent of mountain locals and our cadets jumped from the stands and met in the middle of the court. Lurch was in another zip code. The melee continued for several minutes. Fortunately, there were some police present; they must have expected possible trouble.

The confrontation was brought under control, and we were escorted to the buses. I have never seen so many single-digit hand gestures at one time before or since. The Rabun Gap- Nacoochee police escorted us all the way back to the main gate at RMA in Gainesville.

Following my letter of apology in regard to the incident at Rabun Gap and calls and letters from the staff and coaches, the first half of basketball season was over. We went home for Christmas with a plane ticket to Miami after the holidays. The beach was on the way, and we were excited about the sunny change in January, 1967.

SECOND HALF OF THE YEAR AT THE RMA FLORIDA CAMPUS

It was unbelievably nice in south Florida. The school was in the middle of a major highway that funneled around both sides. The dorms at the Lauderdale campus were much more modern than the RMA residence halls in Georgia. Palm trees were everywhere.

A full-dress parade was held every Sunday in our wool uniforms, not especially comfortable in the warm, deep south Florida climate. I cut the sleeves and bottom out of my dress shirt to be as cool as possible.

In the dorm at RMA in Ft. Lauderdale, we had suite mates, two cadets on each side with a bath to share. Bob Gaskins roomed with me, just as he had in Gainesville, and we were joined by two cadets.

In those days, smoking was allowed if your parents provided written permission at the beginning of the school year. Hard to believe, but true. Bob and I had a suite mate named Farley who was a true chain smoker, one Viceroy after another all day long. It was tough since the smoke obviously did not stay on one side of the suite. Farley's roommate also smoked, but not as much as Farley.

The "River Rats," as we were known, were like walk-ons where ever we went. It did not matter if we were out in public, where we were always in uniform, or on the field or court of play. We were constantly being ridiculed and put down.

After a while, however, we just accepted the fact that we were not liked and moved on. One thing was for sure though: it made you very aware of your need to be always on the lookout for possible trouble.

We traveled in groups of five or six when we had passes to the malls or anywhere outside the walls of the school. I quickly learned that Florida was much worse than Georgia regarding discrimination against those of us in school uniform. I personally believe that is one reason the school sold the Florida property and moved to Georgia full time some years later.

During the second half of our basketball season we played some outstanding basketball teams in the Miami area and managed to finish with a winning record. Now, we were anxious to get started with the baseball season. I played center field, which is much like playing free safety in football, and I really liked the position.

Playing baseball in sunny Florida was a blast! All of our home games were played on one of the New York Yankees' spring training fields, and we saw several of the Yankee players when we were there. The fields were immaculate, and we felt like big leaguers when we stepped out to practice and play.

"PLAIN, OLD FASHIONED HATE"

After playing four or five games and losing only once, the "River Rats" met Miami Pace. It was like Lewis Grizzard, well known UGA humorist and writer, once said about the UGA-Georgia Tech rivalry: it was just "plain, old fashioned hate." That's the way it was between RMA and Miami Pace.

There had been a running mutual dislike between the two schools for years. We played them in basketball earlier and encountered some brief trouble with their fans. Also, a couple of the guys on our team had gotten into an off-campus incident the previous year and that had kept the fires burning.

When Pace arrived there was some immediate "trash talking" and finger-pointing. You could feel the emotion.

Our pitcher was a tall, redhead with a great fastball, but his control was a bit shaky at times. He had a hair trigger of a temper and had a previous history with Pace. Initially, however, the game was non-eventful with routine outs and a hit or two, but no scoring or incidents.

In the fifth inning I got a double with one out and then went to third on a wild pitch. I knew the game would be low scoring and wanted to do what I could to get us a run right then.

The next batter hit a slow roller toward third base, and I took off for home at the crack of the bat. Their catcher, who was built like a stump, took residence on top of home plate when the slow roller was hit. I could see what was about to happen long before "Stump" could since he was focusing on the throw from his third baseman. To make matters worse, the throw was on the first base side of home, and The Stump had to lean away from me as I ran in.

We dressed differently. We had foreign players who spoke differently, and several of our players were African American. It was my first experience of true discrimination and being in the minority.

There was a massive collision. I went in one direction, and "Stump" went in the opposite direction. Ball, glove, mask and whatever else he had that was not attached went in all directions. It looked like a community yard sale in Carrollton, Georgia. on a spring Saturday morning. I scored, and everybody got into the act by converging at home plate. A little pushing and shoving took place, but the umps got it under control.

The very next inning when we were in the field and I was in my usual position in center field "Stump" came to bat. I had a bad feeling about this from the start. I later learned that Stump and our pitcher had a previous history of bad blood.

The first pitch was a fastball for a strike. The next pitch was fouled back. "Stump" was now in a 0-2 hole. The third pitch was a heater just under the chin. "Stump" hit the deck. The fourth pitch came in as hard as I ever saw Red bring it, and it hit "Stump" squarely in the middle of the back. It was like the start of the Boston Marathon. People came from everywhere. Both benches met at the mound. "Stump" took off after Red with a bat in his hand. I ran in from center and got in the middle of it.

We probably had some of the same spectator-cadets there as we did at the melee at Rabun Gap during basketball season. It was a mess like I have never seen before or since. The problem was that it was out of control, and the umps, coaches or anyone else could not get it stopped. It would last a while and start back up. Bats were thrown. How no one was seriously injured was amazing.

Obviously, there were no cell phones back then, so there was there no method to immediately call for help. About 30 minutes after the brawl started, a fire truck rolled in with two six-foot water hoses, and the firemen got things under control. I can still picture "Stump" rolling like a bowling ball as the high-pressure water stream pounded his back.

Order was finally restored. The authorities came and made sure that each team returned home safely. I do not believe RMA played Miami Pace in an athletic event ever again.

Our game with Pace was another example of how things can get out of control when bias and discrimination take over. I do not want to portray RMA as a violent school, because it was not. The school has a solid reputation.

However, the Riverside Military Academy cadets seemed to be viewed as being "different" in the eyes of the locals. We dressed differently. We had foreign players who spoke differently, and several of our players were African American. It was my first experience of true discrimination and being in the minority. It is easy for those in the majority to criticize those who fight

HEADS UP #4

You can not have true faith and worry at the same time.

• 40% of your worries never happen.

• 30% have already happened.

• 12% are health concerns that never happen.

• 10% are concerns about what others think of you.

• 8% may actually be of concern and can be handled.

• Focus on the odds rather than the possibilities.

• Worry looks around. Sorry looks back. Faith looks up.

• The seeds of depression cannot take root in a field of thanksgiving.

• Andy Andrews's *The Noticer,* pages 55-56 are the real deal on worry.

Now faith is being sure of what we hope for and certain of what we cannot see.

– Hebrews 1:11

for minority rights, but when you feel the other side of the issue it puts it all in perspective.

We ended the baseball season at the Florida campus with a very good record and prepared to drive back to Gainesville during spring break.

Arriving on the Gainesville campus in late April, we completed the baseball season with games at Darlington, Baylor, McCauley and several other local schools. We then prepared for the graduation parade in mid-May.

The year-end parade was special, a thing of beauty. Everyone was proud, and it was like we had banded together against some outside opposition and accomplished a goal. With Papa James and Bee attending, it was even greater.

After the ceremony ended and we threw our hats high into the air, I immediately looked for the oldest, nastiest, most torn pair of Levis I could find and retired my uniform forever. However, I still have my dress blues in my closet at this writing.

My year at Riverside Military Academy was now over, and I was ready to go to Athens. We had worked out the details to walk on at the University of Georgia. Colonel McGinnis was very helpful in working with me to arrange the opportunity. But first, I returned home to the hayfield at Rolling Green Farm and worked out every day. During the summer I often wondered how tough it was going to be. It is probably just as well that I did not know.

I think my attitude at the time must have been all about faith in what I believed, even though I cannot say that I had a strong Christian commitment then because I did not. I also believe that others can pray for you and help you, but at some point you have got to turn the radio on and look for the signals. Faith in Jesus Christ is the answer to all worries, concerns and anguish.

V

THE UGA YEARS: 1967
MY FRESHMAN SEASON

With the help of Colonel McGinnis at Riverside Military Academy I set my sights for Athens, Georgia in early August of 1967 following a summer at home on the farm in Ray City.

I carpooled to Athens with Glenn "Barnie" Davis, a consensus all-state quarterback from Valdosta High School and good friend. Barnie and I played Colt League baseball together during the summers at the Valdosta Boys Club.

Arriving at the Coliseum on the UGA campus, we checked in, were fitted for practice gear, and completed the routine physical exam. The next stop was to check in at McWhorter Hall, a new, state-of-the art athletic dorm like nothing I had ever seen in my life. You could see the red doors on the rooms from miles away.

During preseason practice I was assigned a room on the back of McWhorter Hall that was used by the basketball team during the regular school term where I roomed with another walk-on player. All of the front rooms were for the scholarship players and would be their permanent rooms when school started.

While in line to receive my equipment, I had the privilege of meeting Squab Jones, a legend at UGA, who was in charge of issuing and the maintenance of all athletic equipment. Squab had come to Georgia during the Coach Wally Butts era and remained there many years later. He was hard-nosed but dedicated and fair. Although Squab was black and there was discrimination in our society, he never let it get in his way regarding his authority. Mr. Beavers was a great guy and was in charge of the department, but he let Squab run the show.

We began two-a-day practices the day after we arrived in Athens, and I was like a fish out of water. I began my career at UGA as the number four wide receiver on the freshman team that was comprised of about 65 players. I was one of about 25 walk-ons, most of whom were good athletes, but were undersized. The majority of the players who were low on the depth charts comprised the scout team and were used to hold dummies during practice.

FROM HOLDING DUMMIES TO STARTING SAFETY

Each player had a masking tape strip on the front of his helmet with his name printed in magic marker. Although my name was misspelled as "Swindel," I was seldom acknowledged during the two-a-days, so I let the error slide since my name did not matter much.

A fellow freshman whom I really admired was James Hurley, a defensive end and a good player. He was black and, as far as I know, was the first African-American to ever suit up on the practice fields of UGA. James was a hitter and had great courage, especially considering the time. The Civil Rights Act of 1964 was relatively new, and few of us white guys had accepted its meaning. Most of us thought the all black Texas Western University (now Texas-El Paso) basketball team that won NCAA National Basketball Champs the year before in 1966 was a fluke.

Although African American players were being signed in the Southeastern Conference at Tennessee, Kentucky, and Florida, in 1967, UGA was four years away from signing its first black player, Horace King, to an athletic scholarship. I had the privilege of coaching the secondary as a grad assistant on that team in 1971. That class featured the Bulldogs' first five scholarship African American players, including Larry West, a speedy corner and a great young man, whom I had the privilege to coach.

But in 1967, arriving at UGA as a walk-on freshman, I was far from being a college football player. I quickly discovered that the speed, size, and depth of quality players were beyond anything I had imagined. It was especially evident when the varsity came down to scrimmage the freshman team.

Standing around, holding a practice dummy, and filling in wherever I was needed was how I spent most of my time during preseason practice. Frankly though, I was just plain happy to be where I was. I felt like I was part of the team, but there were many more obstacles ahead. In 1967 freshman eligibility for varsity play was five years away.

We had some great coaches on the Georgia Bullpup freshman team in 1967. Coach Doc Ayers, a native of Toccoa, Georgia and a state championship football coach at Cedartown High School, was our head coach. A true "players' coach," he was always honest with his players and very fair to me.

Not too long ago, my good friend Harvey Copeland of Carrollton and I had a chance to have lunch with Coach Ayers in Cedartown where he has lived for many years. It was great seeing and talking with him and that meeting brought back many good memories.

Coach John Donaldson, a Jesup, Georgia. native and All American halfback at UGA in the 40's, also was a freshman coach. He was an inspirational leader with his constant "Hubba-Hubbas" and firm, confident smile.

Stay the course if it's the correct course.

• Make sure you can measure the results in whatever you do.

• Change always has a price tag.

• The best way to dig yourself out of a hole is first to stop digging.

• Make sure you remember that God made a windshield a lot bigger than a rearview mirror.

Blessed is the man who perseveres under trial, because when he has stood the test of time he will receive the crown of life that God has promised to those who love Him.

– James 1:12

Joe Burson and Bob Taylor, who were seniors on the 1966 UGA team, served as our graduate assistant coaches. Coach Burson was the first coach who really took time to work with me individually. It gave me a needed boost in confidence at a time when I needed it.

Our freshman team schedule consisted of six games with our major rivals, culminated by the annual Thanksgiving Game at Georgia Tech. I played in every game on special teams, but, oddly enough, did not play a single down from scrimmage until the first snap at Grant Field on Thanksgiving Day when I started at free safety.

Following the freshman game against Florida and the week before the season ending game at Georgia Tech, Coach Burson suggested to Coach Ayers that I be given a shot at free safety. Frankly, I was not making any progress at the receiver position, and there was a need for more depth in the secondary as we approached the final game of the season against Tech.

The move to safety was good for me, although I do not believe there have been many free safeties who wore the #87. But that was my number, and I was proud of it. I was convinced that I was in the right position. Moving to number four on the depth chart at receiver to the number three free safety on the freshman team made me feel that I was finally being recognized as a player.

MEMORABLE VISIT TO SCOTTISH RITE

One of the most fortunate circumstances I can remember in my life occurred prior to the season ending game at Georgia Tech. We had played five games in front of sparse crowds, which was common for freshmen contests, and were in game-week preparation for the meeting with the Yellow Jackets. At the time the Georgia-Georgia Tech freshman game was a major event. Played each season in Atlanta at Tech's Grant Field on Thanksgiving Day, the game was attended by thousands of fans. All proceeds were donated to the Scottish Rite Children's Hospital in Atlanta.

Our quarterback on the freshman team was Mike Cavan, an outstanding high school player at Thomaston High School. Mike, with whom I roomed during our junior season, would later become a successful Division I football coach at several schools. When serving as an assistant coach at UGA 13 years later in 1980, he gained fame for recruiting and signing the great Herschel Walker.

Mike turned his ankle against Florida prior to our final game of the season with Tech. Coach Ayers decided not to take a chance on Mike's injury and did not list him on the game roster. Jack Montgomery, a high school All-American from Moultrie, was the freshman team starting free safety and was also the second team quarterback. With Mike's injury, Jack was now the starting QB, a change that moved me to the number two free safety position behind John Griffin.

But John, an All State player from St. Pius High School in Atlanta, had problems with hamstring injuries throughout his football career at UGA. As fate would have it he pulled his nagging hamstring on Monday at practice prior to our trip to Atlanta on Thursday. John made every effort to play through the injury, but there was just no way.

Coach Burson was now down to the last few defensive backs on the team, so I was sure he would go to one of the scholarship players on offense and find someone to play safety since I had not played a down from the line of scrimmage in a game the entire season.

When John went down on Monday Coach Burson, Coach Taylor, and Coach Ayers huddled up as all the players stood around and wondered: what now? I will never forget what happened next. Coach Ayers came directly over to me and put his arm around my # 87 as I was preparing myself to hear his decision to select a scholarship player from offense to start in front of me. That did not happen. His words to me were, "You have hung in well and have been learning this position. Coach Burson and I are in agreement. You will start at free safety against Georgia Tech this Thursday at Grant Field."

I was shocked when Coach Ayers told me that I would start against Tech in the biggest game of the season. I was the last man standing, so to speak, and they were placing their trust in me. I really was not a devout Christian at the time, but I do remember stepping into that number one defensive huddle for the first time at practice and looking up at the clouds and thanking God for giving me this huge opportunity.

I think I was like many other people at some stage in their lives. I just got caught up in my own personal agenda and sort of worked around Christ. It is so easy to treat the Lord as convenience allows. Many people must have physical evidence of spirituality and give themselves the credit for their accomplishments. Learning to love Christ at a young age and becoming involved in Christian youth activities such as The Fish House, Big Stuff and Mission Outreach are key to forming a strong spiritual foundation.

There were people in the defensive huddle at practice that day who I did not know. I had to memorize their names from the masking tape on their helmets. As for my own helmet tape that had featured the misspelling of my name throughout preseason practice and our freshman schedule, I removed the name tape and wrote in the correct spelling of "Swindle."

I was now the only walk-on lining up with the starting defense. I had been studying the defensive system from the sidelines all season, and I knew the schemes well. We played a Split 60 Defense that legendary Coach Erk Russell, our varsity assistant head coach and defensive coordinator, brought with him to UGA from his tenure at Auburn.

Our base defense required the safety to be able to cover a lot of ground, especially to the deep outside. Since I was tall and rangy I could make that play in the seam. The only time the safety played man-to-man was in the blitz calls, and usually the second inside receiver on the strong side was covered by the safety. However, man-to-man coverage was not my strength. Later in my career some opposing coaches noticed man defense was not my strong suit, so they set up in a wide slot formation in which the wide slot put the tight end on the backside of the formation and the slot receiver, usually the best and fastest receiver, as the second inside receiver on the strong side. That put the best receiver on the least effective cover guy. Get the picture! I did not like the wide slot formation, especially when we had a man blitz called.

With only two full practices behind me as the starting safety, we bused to Atlanta on Wednesday for the Thanksgiving Classic. Since the game was played on behalf of the Scottish Rite Children's Hospital, each team visited the hospital the day before. I had never seen anything like what I experienced that day. There were kids with severe physical disabilities, terminal illnesses, and all types of problems.

Tentative at first, I quickly noticed that the kids were very happy to see us. Their attitudes were upbeat and so positive. I never was the same after that day. Even though I was not in tune with God's plan at the time, the experience at Scottish Rite Children's Hospital changed my outlook on life forever.

I recall a beautiful six-year old girl with terminal leukemia who asked me for my signature on her Bulldog visor. It was the first time that anyone had ever asked me for an autograph.

Good health is so fragile and unpredictable, but we can do much to improve our chances of good health. I think God expects us to do what we can to promote good health and safety in our lives. The trip to Scottish Rite gave me a new outlook on the appreciation of a sound, healthy body. I think of those children often and all those who have benefited by the treatment at such a fantastic facility.

I still feel a point of pride when I remember my participation in the Georgia–Georgia Tech Freshman Thanksgiving Classic over 44 years ago that benefited the Scottish Rite Children's Hospital, now known as Children's Healthcare of Atlanta.

My first game as a UGA starter, wearing #87, was at Grant Field in Atlanta in the annual Thanksgiving Day Freshman Classic game in 1967. Alongside is fellow walk-on #47 Vic Belloite, an all-state linebacker from Dublin, Georgia.

LAST MAN STANDING

Thursday was Game Day, and I think every butterfly at Callaway Gardens was in my stomach as we suited up to play Tech. The fans were pouring in and eventually filled the stadium. It was raining a bit, but the weather did not keep the crowd away.

Bee and Papa James sat in the lower level on the Georgia side where I could clearly see them. Coach Ayers gave a pep talk that raised the hair on everyone's neck, and out we went. I really had a good feeling as we ran on the field. Once we broke a sweat in the warm-up some of butterflies were released.

I had never played before such a large crowd, and I was curious how good the Tech guys were. What amazed me the most about my first experience in a competitive collegiate game was how much faster everyone was as compared to a typical practice. The emotion and adrenaline rush makes a huge difference on game day, but I think the old saying, "You will play like you practice," is the prevailing truth. I was prepared, and I had a good game. It was not a great performance, but I did not make any glaring mistakes. I made some plays in the secondary and even made a few tackles.

Tech won the game 14-0, but Coach Ayers was not unhappy with our effort, and he said so after the game. I will never forget him coming up to me in the locker room as we were getting ready to leave for Athens and saying, "You were the last man standing, and you did a damn good job."

Even though Coach Ayers was referring to the fact I was the only safety without an injury at the time, I think his support at that time provided me with some much needed encouragement. When I look back on playing in the game against Tech I can only believe that God wanted me to have that chance. I know there was a strong signal sent to me, and the impact of the trip to Scottish Rite remains with me to this day.

1968 – AN SEC CHAMPIONSHIP SEASON

The 1968 football season at the University of Georgia for Buck Swindle almost became the season that never was.

Once my freshman season was over I focused on off-season workouts and getting ready for spring practice as one of approximately 15 walk-ons who were invited to participate. Spring practice was to begin in April. However, I gradually began to feel disenchanted with my life at UGA. Over the winter, the euphoria of starting and playing well in the last game of my freshman season against Georgia Tech had begun to wane. Shortly before the end of winter quarter I decided that the University of Georgia and Bulldog football were not for me.

I had been talking with Rhett Dawson, a good friend with whom I had grown up in the Valdosta-Ray City area. Rhett, a standout at Valdosta High, was now at Florida State University where he would go on to an All-America career as a Seminole receiver. Following a trip to Tallahassee where Rhett introduced me to the FSU coaches who reviewed the film of my performance in the freshman game against Georgia Tech, I was offered a partial athletic grant to attend Florida State. Although the partial scholarship was actually only slightly more than the out-of-state tuition, I was pleased to have been offered by Florida State. I had been less than enthusiastic with the reception that I had received from the UGA coaches during winter workouts.

I was to officially sign with FSU on a Monday when I was scheduled to arrive for their spring practice. I had already withdrawn from UGA without notifying the coaches, not that they would have lost a minute's sleep over it. I even pledged a jock fraternity at FSU and had the sticker on my back window.

I was set to go to Florida State and had my car packed on the Sunday night prior to my leaving from the farm in Ray City for Tallahassee the next day. UGA spring practice was to start on Wednesday of the same week, but I would not be there. I was headed to Florida State. That Sunday night while talking to my mother, Bee, she asked me if I was sure about my decision to not return to Athens and go to Florida State. I told her that I was sure. It was what I wanted to do.

But over the next few hours, I began thinking about my decision and had a change of heart. I called Rhett and told him that I was backing out and would remain at UGA. Rhett was disappointed, but it was done. To this day I am sure God spoke to me that Sunday night. It was a decision that was to change the course of my life.

I had decided to return to Georgia, but I was still in a mess. I was not enrolled for spring quarter, and I had no place to live. The dorms were full and freshmen could not live off campus. But I had made my decision. I climbed in my Carolina blue Olds 442 with the FSU Chi Phi sticker in the rear window early on Monday morning and headed to Athens.

On the way to Athens, I called my old Valdosta friend, Mo Thrash, who was a student at UGA. I had known Mo for several years, and he had invited me to several parties at the Pi Kappa Alpha house. I asked him if he had any ideas as to where I might live for a few days until a dorm cancellation came available. Mo, after talking with another Valdosta-UGA fraternity brother, Barry Henry, told me to come to the Pi Kappa

Alpha house Monday night, and we would figure something out. That night I slept in the upper loft of the Pike House. The night turned into the entire spring quarter, as no dorms became available.

I re-enrolled in school without a problem, and the Pike guys put me on the "Modified American Plan" which included a meal ticket if I bused tables and did wash detail in the fraternity house. It was a done deal, but had to be under the radar. We definitely stretched the rules on that one, and those guys went out on a limb for me. I will always be thankful to them.

I reported for the first day of spring practice as if nothing had changed. No coach or player knew what had transpired, as if anyone would have really cared at the time.

Spring practice included 28 sessions in pads, the G-Day Spring Game, and two additional days of practice after G-Day. The first two weeks of practice were like hell on earth for me. Once again, like those first days when I reported as a walk-on freshman, I was a fish out of water.

I knew the 1967 varsity was good, but I had no idea just how talented and mature the '68 team was going to be. A few months later this team would be Southeastern Conference Champions and ranked fourth in the final polls. It would feature about 15 seniors, most of whom were fifth year players, eight All-SEC players, and four All-Americans. Five years later, two members of that '68 team would be stars on the undefeated NFL Champion Miami Dolphins of 1972. This group was the real deal. I am glad that I did not know just how good they were at the time.

We began practice with drills emphasizing fundamentals. One of the drills was known in football terms as the "Inside and Outside Oklahoma." On offense the drill featured a center, quarterback, fullback, running back, and right and left guard. The defense included two linemen, two linebackers and two defensive backs. Simply stated, the inside call was up the middle, and the outside call was a sweep outside. Only the offense knew the call, and the defense had to react and tackle.

The use of the Oklahoma Drill was an effective tool to determine the strength and ability of players very quickly. It also appeared to be useful in discouraging non-scholarship players from continued participation.

I failed to mention that success at tackling the ball carrier was also mandatory for each defensive player, and each failure required another opportunity. I was absolutely the worst tackler on the football field, and the more I was required to try, the worse I was and the more determined the staff was to get rid of me. I am surprised my arms were not torn from my body since I thought grabbing was acceptable. I have never been so humiliated in my life. I was going up against varsity players who made me look like a fool. I can remember the coaches and players laughing at me after so many repeated misses that I was finally told to "get in the back of the line."

This situation lasted for about 12 days without any improvement. My face was pretty banged up, and I ached all over.

At the end of practice one day Coach Kinard, the varsity secondary coach, asked me, "Is all this worth it? What are you doing here?"

Was I regretting my decision to return to Athens and continue my role in the Bulldog football program? You bet I was!

I showered that day and went to my "secret home" in the loft of the Pi Kappa Alpha house. There was just enough room for a cot and one table.

After Day Fourteen of spring practice I was a wreck. I did not shower after practice and just took the old 442 to the house with one stop at a local beverage location. I was hurting in every inch on my body, especially my ribs on the right side. A deep breath would curl my toes. I did not see any way to make it any longer. I was ready to quit.

I got the guys together at the fraternity house, and after a few supporting libations and some "hey come on and party with us and forget all that BS," I was convinced. The time had come to leave UGA football for good.

THE CALL THAT KEPT ME A BULLDOG

First, however, I had to make one phone call. I called home, and Papa James answered. I began to explain how I was being abused both emotionally and physically, and there was no way I could continue. I just needed one ounce of reinforcement.

Papa James did not respond immediately. Following a pause he said, "Let me get your mother."

Pop got Bee on the phone, and I went through what I hoped would be an even more convincing explanation with her on why I thought I needed to quit football. I thought to myself: what mother would not understand and support her son's position regarding his health and well being?

Bee listened, but she did not immediately respond. I thought we had been disconnected at first.

"Let me call you back in just a minute," she said as she rather abruptly hung up.

I wondered why Bee would not immediately support my position. Five minutes later, the phone rang and Bee asked me, "What time does practice start each day?"

I thought to myself: what a bizarre question to ask. I responded: "It starts at 3 o'clock."

I really thought I had convinced her that, in my opinion, the coaches were not spending time working with me at spring practice because they really wanted me to quit.

Bee paused and then asked me if I could find someone on the team who could help me with my problem. She also listed every single accomplishment that I had made on the football field since I started playing in the ninth grade. She concluded by asking me to stick it out another "day or two" while I tried to find someone to talk to who might be able to help and then call her back. I could not believe my ears. I was blown away to say the least.

I went to bed before dark that night and did not make a single class the next day because of trips to the drug store to buy some Creamalgesic ointment. I rubbed and whirl-pooled in the training room at the Coliseum for most of the day.

JAKE SCOTT CAME TO MY RESCUE

The following day at about 1 p.m., I was sitting on the bench next to my locker when I noticed three senior players walking down the hall. I thought to myself, "Why would those guys be here this early?" As it turned out they were returning from a "visit" to Coach Vince Dooley's office. I immediately recognized one of the players as Jake Scott, the first team All-SEC free safety from the past season and a consensus pre-season All-American. I decided that I had to speak up now. This was my chance.

"Hey Jake," I said.

"How 'bout it," he answered as he stopped to talk to me.

I told Jake that I needed some help, and he responded by asking me if I needed a ride somewhere. Jake didn't recognize me as a player, walk-on that I was, even though I had walked past him every day for months.

I said, "No, don't need a ride. I'm Buck Swindle, a freshman safety out for spring practice."

"Yeah, I know who you are. You're the one featured in the Big Drill,"

Jake Scott in 1968 was an All-SEC and All-American safety. He went on to become a star on the only unbeaten team in NFL history, the 1972 Miami Dolphins, on which he was the Super Bowl MVP. Jake was recently named to the College Football Hall of Fame.

Jake said in reference to the "Oklahoma" drill.

"Man, you don't have a clue," he added. "Well what do you need? I am in a bit of a rush."

I had a lump in my throat, but I asked him to help me with my open field tackling, since I had not made one in 14 consecutive days, and the coaches seemed to have given up on me and wanted me to quit.

"You just need to have an extra session or two on that dumbass Okie Drill," he replied.

Jake went on to explain that the safety position is for guys who can get to the deep outside and make plays in the seam. He told me that the Southeastern Conference was 75 percent pass and 25 percent run, and four of the best passing quarterbacks on the planet were in the SEC.

"I guess those coaches believe you need to be able to tackle before you can be considered a defender," he added. "Makes sense I guess, especially for a walk-on nobody knows."

Then Jake paused for a moment.

"Ahh, whatever. What the ----. I got some time. See you on the field at 2 o'clock," he said.

It was like I had been totally rejuvenated. In 30 minutes of personal training from Jake Scott, I not only learned about tackling and playing the free safety position, but I also learned what it means to be helped by someone in a tough time. Jake's philosophy was much like my mother's mantra: keep it simple and repeat positive thoughts.

JAKE'S WAY

#1-You have to break down and get yourself under control.

#2- You have to be willing to give ground.

#3-Always follow the heart. The number on the front of the jersey hides the heart.

#4-Look in their eyes for the truth.

Jake was one of the best ever when it came to anticipation. He focused on reading the quarterback's eyes to give him the advantage. He said the last place the QB looks is usually where the play goes. Watch the eyes. Therein lies the truth

This was all we ever talked about. It was a matter of some drills and positive thoughts that made the difference. The turning point came when Jake approached me after I had made three consecutive successful tackles in an "Okie Drill" and said to me, "You can play this position. Just follow me for a while and execute the basics."

That experience with Jake transformed my life in so many ways. My confidence level skyrocketed. It was like a light came on in the deepest darkness. If you can imagine, just a few days before the end of spring practice, I actually looked forward to the "Okie Drill." I moved from the lowest level on the depth chart to number four. Now it was time for the selection of players of who were going to play in the G-Day Game, the intra-squad game that ended spring practice.

I am relatively sure that Jake had a "ding" (minor injury) and that's why he asked to skip the G-Day Game. Therefore, with a smaller number of safeties from which to choose, I was designated to start for the Red Team at free safety. It was quite a turnaround from a few weeks before when I was so discouraged that I wanted to quit.

Prior to the game, Coach Kinard asked me if I had returned punts before. I must admit that I stretched the truth a bit when I said, "Yeah, sure. No problem."

In reality I had never returned a punt in my life at any level, but I wanted every possible advantage I could muster to get a scholarship.

During the year I had become good friends with Spike Jones of Louisville, Georgia. Spike, a former walk-on, was now an All-SEC punter and would later become a standout for seven years in the NFL, but on this day he was designated as punter for the Black team in the G-Day Game.

Spike and I met and discussed the upcoming game. I had caught hundreds of his punts over the past year, and I was aware of his awesome hang time and ability to punt the football for distance, especially into the wind. He hardly ever outkicked his coverage and that is what made him so valuable as a punter in college and the NFL.

When we met and talked about being on opposite sides for the G-Day Game, he asked me if I had ever seen his "rocket kick" that was low and long. No, I answered—not often— always long and high with fair catch written all over it. He then casually mentioned that I should line up a bit deeper and be ready when Black Team punted to my Red Team.

God gives us signs– keep the radio on and tuned to the right channel.

- Prayer creates the spiritual conduit to receive divine guidance.

- When you get the signal, take action and make decisions based on wisdom.

- The main thing is to make the main thing the main thing. Focus.

Show me thy ways O Lord, teach me your paths, guide me in your truth and teach me for you are God my Savior and my hope is in you all the day long.

– Psalms 25:4-5

It was time for the game at Sanford Stadium, and there was a good crowd of about 10,000. The first time that Spike's Black Team had to punt, I disregarded his tip to line up deeper than the normal 40 yards downfield from the line of scrimmage. Spike kicked it well over my head, but I luckily caught it like making a Willie Mays-type basket catch in baseball.

After bringing the ball in I turned to the wall of blockers that was called to be set up on the left side. The wall was set up perfectly, and I had a head of steam. Spike was the last guy who could have gotten to me, and he took his shot. But I gave my best juke move and scored. I will always remember the smile on Spike's face when I ran past him. While Spike already had his scholarship and was well on his way to SEC honors and NFL stardom, for me it was my "coming out party." Spike and I have remained close friends through the years, and I appreciate his friendship very much. Just in case I did not tell Spike at the Seagraves Party, I want to thank him for the rocket kick. Better late than never!

Actually, the G-Day Game in the spring of 1968 was in many ways the game of my life. I had one or maybe two interceptions, the punt return for a TD and actually made some open field tackles. I was beside myself after the game and believed that a scholarship would be coming my way soon. Not so, as things turned out.

We had a great "Seagraves Party," a small pig pickin' and refreshment offering for players-only following spring practice every year. Several infamous events resulted from that memorable event. Legend has it that Jake rode one of this Harley's over the Coliseum from front to back after one of those "black tie" events. I did not see him do it, but I did notice bars were added some time after the rumor broke.

BACK HOME ON THE FARM

School ended, and it was back home in the hay field and farm work. I really enjoyed being back home and working with Papa James. Pop and Bee were proud that I had stuck things out and did well during the last half of spring practice.

I had a quiet moment one night after an all day square- bale day at the farm, and I told Bee how much I appreciated her "off the wall advice" during the phone call from the frat house in Athens. She kind of laughed and gave me a big hug without a word. She was and is a lady of few words with a defined meaning. Bee is an angel appointed by our Lord and Savior for sure!

The summer of '68 went by like a wind of destiny. We harvested the tobacco and square-baled hay like gangbusters. Rhett Dawson was home from FSU, and he and I worked a good bit on the farm and found time to work out one-on-one. I could never cover him on an island, but it was great to give it a go. FSU was really well beyond other teams in offensive schemes at that time. I know Rhett and Papa James had some good times on the farm in my absence, but it was always a pleasure to have us all together.

During the summer I was excited to receive weekly reports regarding daily summer workouts from one of the greatest coaches of all time, Erskine Russell, UGA assistant head coach and defensive coordinator. I had no reason to believe that I was not part of the team since I was receiving the same communications as all the other players and was being required to follow the same workout schedules.

In addition to working out together almost every day, Rhett and I were invited on several occasions by Valdosta High's legendary coach Wright Bazemore to come to the Wildcats' football camp at Twin Lakes. What a great experience that was.

As the summer progressed there was still no word from Athens as to the possibility of me being awarded a football scholarship. Calls to Coach Dooley's office regarding my status had not been returned. Although I received another offer from Florida State, we were sure that UGA would come through. We wanted that to happen.

With the start of fall practice only a week away, I had no dorm arrangements and no scholarship offer at UGA. We had waited much too long for a decision.

Around 6 p.m. on Sunday, July 28, 1968, Papa James made a phone call from the privacy of his bedroom to Coach Vince Dooley. I never knew the content of the conversation and was never told. Following his brief talk with Coach Dooley, Papa James told me to pack my bags and be ready at 4 a.m. to leave for Athens.

Shortly after arriving at Coach Vince Dooley's office at 9 a.m., I signed a full scholarship to play football for the University of Georgia Bulldogs. Since I signed on the 29th of July, I requested jersey #29, and my request was granted.

Looking back on that eventful day over 40 years ago, I obviously am thankful to many people in my life. A special thanks goes to Jake Scott, but also to Spike Jones, and Mark Stewart, who worked with me when Jake was otherwise occupied. "Craze," which was Mark's nickname, was a wonderful friend and is greatly missed.

This is a appropriate time during these recollections to offer my thanks to Mo Thrash, Barry Henry, Billy Ozier, and the other Pi Kappa Alpha guys who allowed me to stow away at their house during the spring of '68 when my life was very much in limbo. I was later initiated as a PKA.

My thanks also go to the coaches at UGA who believed in me and later allowed me to start in 22 consecutive SEC games as a Georgia Bulldog and receive a SEC Championship ring in the process. I also owe thanks to my friend, Rhett Dawson, and to all the coaches at FSU, whose interest in me was a great confidence booster. To this day, my entire family shows their loyalty to the 'Noles by being good-natured "Gator Haters."

Of most importance, my deepest gratitude goes to my father, Papa James, and my mother, Bee, for steering me in the right direction at a time when the train was off the track. I will never forget the look on Bee's face as I walked with the team by family, friends, and fans and down the cross tie steps to the Sanford Stadium entrance for our first game in 1968. Wow!

PRE-SEASON PRACTICE STARTS FOR THE 1968 SEASON

I could not believe the reception that I received when I reported to McWhorter Hall. It had been just less than a year since I lived there for a few weeks as a walk-on freshman. Now I truly felt that this was my place to belong.

In retrospect, I wish that I had been better connected spiritually then and had a local church commitment as a top priority. But I didn't. I was caught up in the thrill of being a UGA Bulldog.

The first order of business after getting physical exams was running a mile for time around the two practice fields that were set end to end. Backs and linebackers had to make it in at least six minutes and linemen in six and a half.

The weekly letters that we received during the summer emphasized the importance of "making the mile." It was indicative of how committed each player was to the summer workout program and to the success of the season. The players who did not "make the mile" had to get up at 5 a.m. and run it again for time with a grumpy coach using a suspect stop watch.

Running a six-minute mile is a modified sprint. I ran with Spike and finished with something near a 5:30. Spike was well ahead of me and won the event. Most everyone fell out after the finish and fed the fish.

It was evident from the start that the '68 team had awesome talent, maturity, and depth. The coaches told us that most, if not all, the incoming sophomores would be redshirted. "Craze" Stewart was Jake Scott's backup at safety, but he also was the starting left cornerback. Therefore, I was technically the number three safety at the beginning of two-a-days.

I was elevated to number two safety when John Griffin sustained the first of many hamstring pulls. A week away from the opener at the University of Tennessee in Knoxville I was also getting frequent work on special teams. For some reason Jake missed a good bit of practice time, and I occasionally practiced with the starting defensive unit.

MY FIRST VARSITY GAME – UT IN KNOXVILLE

We flew to Knoxville on two Southern Airways DC-9 jets. The starting offensive and defensive teams flew on one plane, and the number two O and D on the other.

Arriving at Neyland Stadium I was like a Kansas farm boy walking down 5th Avenue in New York for the first time. All I could do was look up at all that orange and say "Gaah-lee!" I had never seen anything like it in my life. The sheer number of orange people was amazing.

It was a super hot September day, and to make matters worse, Tennessee had just installed something called "Tartan Turf." Tartan Turf was supposed to be the finest synthetic athletic surface on the planet. Actually, it proved to the best heat reflector (115 degrees on the field that day) and the most prolific cause of multiple staph infections on the planet. In fact, following the game we had 15-20 cases of serious staph infections that were said to be caused by abrasions received by our players in the game. I am sure that the UGA administration dealt with the issue directly, because UT took the infected carpet out soon afterwards.

The game was back and forth. Bruce Kemp went 80 yards on a dive play.

Jake took a long punt to the house and had a one-handed interception. We took a 17-9 lead late into the fourth quarter. Our pressure split 60 defense had been working great.

However, during the waning moments the Vols managed to drive the ball to our 34 where they had a fourth and one with nine seconds left. And then the call that I hated more than any other came in ---Victory D. Victory D is designed to lengthen the defense and eliminate the chance for a long, big play. In reality it causes the defense to relax and lose intensity.

The UT quarterback, Bobby Scott, threw a floater to the corner of the end zone, and their receiver made a great catch to make the score 17-15 as time expired. The two point play was a nightmare. The official who made the call had to have been a relative of the ref who made the infamous excessive celebration call against A.J. Green in the 2009 loss to LSU. It was the worst call I had ever seen.

Since I signed on the 29th of July, I requested jersey #29, and my request was granted.
PHOTO PROVIDED BY THE UNIVERSITY OF GEORGIA DEPARTMENT OF SPORTS COMMUNICATIONS

Going for two to tie the game, Scott threw to the tight end over the middle, and he went to his knees and made a great catch--- after the ball had bounced off the infected carpet. But the ref ruled it a legal catch. Their fans and our sidelines went nuts for opposite reasons as the game ended in a 17-17 tie. Overtime periods were many years away. What an ending to my first game.

I had never seen one of those high dollar Rydell helmets break before or since, but Jake split his in half on the inside block wall of the visitor locker room. I have never seen such a furious, dejected group of players.

But in retrospect, the heartbreaking last second tie at Tennessee added several extra layers of toughness on everybody, especially with several players who had boils treated and lanced the following week as a result of the abrasions caused by the infamous Tartan Turf.

A VERY SPECIAL DAY

Following the disheartening tie against the Volunteers in the 1968 season opener at Knoxville, my first game at Sanford Stadium as a member of the Bulldog varsity came in Game Two when we hosted our border rival, the Clemson Tigers.

Before the east-train trestle end of Sanford Stadium was enclosed it was a tradition for the team to depart the buses from the Coliseum to the stadium and walk down a long set of cross tie steps before entering the stadium locker room. Lining the steps were cheering Dog fans who extended their hands and shouted words of support and encouragement. The experience sent chills down the spine of every player who has ever had that unique opportunity.

As I walked down the old cross ties for the first time, I saw Bee near the bottom of the steps. She was standing there with her lunch box purse labeled with my #29, a cherished treasure that I have in my office today. Pop was standing off to the side. It was a special day and time in my life that I will never forget. I can to this day see the smile on her face.

Following a 31-13 win in Athens over Clemson, we went to hostile Columbia, SC to play the South Carolina Gamecocks. After quickly falling behind 13-0 less than two minutes into the game we rallied and won a close one, 21-20. Coach Dooley had to wear a helmet to prevent injury from random barrages of most certainly empty Jack Daniels bottles hurled by South Carolina fans. Never before or since have I seen a coach wear a helmet during a game.

Coach Dooley used only four true sophomores on the '68 team. Billy Darby, Mike Cavan, Billy Brice, and I were the members of that true sophomore foursome who went on to letter and earn SEC championship rings. The balance of the class was redshirted.

Billy Darby and I played on special teams, and he was our "nickel back" in our so called "Victory" defense. Victory usually meant a win for the other guy. I hated it when we had been holding an opponent all day and then had to back up and give them the underneath stuff. That "Victory" defense costs us the Tennessee game.

JAKE'S PLEA

Jake privately pleaded with the coaches to not play Billy Darby or me unless someone was injured. Jake's reasoning was that unless Billy and I were really needed to fill in for someone who was hurt we could be redshirted and save a year of eligibility. Honestly though, I wanted to play as soon as possible and so did Billy. In any case, the decision was made to play us both, despite Jake's plea.

I have wondered since that time how things would have played out if Billy had been redshirted that season and had competed as a fifth year senior three years later in the 1971 when we played Auburn for the SEC Championship. With a redshirt season in '68, Billy Darby would have been covering Auburn's All-America receiver Terry Beasley.

As a graduate assistant working the defense from the press box, I remember the Dogs were in Coach Wyant's cover-two defense when Beasley caught a short hook pass from their All-America and later Heisman Trophy winning quarterback Pat Sullivan. Our safety, the position that Billy would have been playing that day, hit Beasley up high, but did not lock up. Beasley made a spin move and went 80 yards for a TD that won Auburn the SEC title. That was a pivotal play that, in my opinion, clinched it for Sullivan in winning the Heisman Trophy a couple of weeks later.

Would have things turned out differently if Billy Darby had been out there? Let's just say that every year when Coach Sullivan goes to New York to attend the Heisman presentation, he needs to send Bill Darby a thank-you note.

ON A ROLL AND A GLIMPSE OF THE FUTURE

Following the win at South Carolina, we went on a roll, easily whipping Ole Miss, Vandy, and Kentucky. Then the Houston Cougars came to Athens.

Houston was the real deal in those days. Coach Bill Yeomans had invented the famous Split Back Veer Offense, but he was also recognized for his outstanding development and use of tremendous black skill players. Both things were to have a tremendous impact on college football. Two of his most well known black players who we faced that day at Sanford Stadium were powerful, lightening fast Elmo Wright and Paul Gipson.

We probably should have been blown out by the powerful Houston team, but the Veer was a high risk offense, and in that game I believe the

Cougars fumbled the ball seven times. It was more like a track meet than a football game. Elmo was blowing by Penny Pennington and "Craze" like a rocket. Jake was playing 18 yards deep all day and still had trouble running him down. It was impossible to take the pitch man on the option and play man on Elmo at the same time. Gipson was a great running back and was later a first round choice of the Atlanta Falcons.

The Cougars could run and throw at will between the 20's, but were severely handicapped when they put it on the ground seven times inside the red zone. Jake also picked off a tipped pass once when they were inside the 20.

We were only down by three, 10-7, going into the fourth quarter. We managed to drive close enough for a long field goal attempt by Jim McCollough. Jim was a very accurate kicker, but distance was sometimes a challenge for him.

But not this time. Jim drilled a 48-yarder into the breeze, and we somehow pulled out a tie. To my knowledge that was Jim's longest career field goal. We were fortunate that day in getting the 10-10 tie, our second of the season, and were glad to see the Cougars get on the plane and return to Houston.

Looking back on that game against Houston in 1968 and the skills and speed of their black players it was, in a way, a glimpse into the future. I still wonder why it took the UGA program three more years to sign its first black football player. Frankly though, I guess I should be glad since I might have lost my starting position for the next two years.

THE ROUT OF THE FLORIDA GATORS IN A HURRICANE

The Georgia-Florida game in 1968 was a swamp in the literal sense. We arrived in Jacksonville on Friday, and it began to "drizzle" a bit in the early morning. We went to the stadium for a light workout but did not stay long. The rain increased, and we were informed that a late hurricane was due to make landfall during the night.

The rain was constant and heavy for hours. I roomed with Jack Montgomery from Moultrie, and we thought for a while that the game might be postponed. But it went on as scheduled while the downpour continued unabated Saturday morning and through kickoff off at 3:30. Despite the deluge, the stands were packed.

From our sideline, however, it was like there was no rain at all as we quickly jumped out to a 24-0 lead. In the middle of the first quarter Coach

Dooley screamed, "Jet Team! Jet Team! Jet Team!" It was the signal for the number two defense and number two offense to get ready to play. I came in and replaced Jake, and it was our game from that point on.

On my third play we were in a man blitz. The Gator slot receiver ran an out, but the pass was tipped at the line. I cut in, picked it off, and sloshed it back about 30 yards. I should have taken my first interception all the way, but I began to hydroplane on the flooded field and ended up under the Gator bench on my backside.

That year Jake set a new all-time SEC record for interceptions in one season with 10. I gave him a run on that record my next year with eight.

It is amazing to me that Terry Hogue, former UGA All-American, broke the record a few years later with 12 in a single season. I am not sure how the records were kept regarding bowl statistics, but I believe Jake had 16 career interceptions in only two years. I ended my career with 14 in three years.

As the game ended and the scoreboard showing 51-0, the largest margin of victory in the history of the series, you could barely see the Florida players on the opposite side of the field because of the torrential rain. There was no need for bourbon mixers that day. Just pour and hold the cup to the sky. I saw that first hand on the way out the tunnel after the game ended.

PLAYING AT AUBURN FOR THE SEC CHAMPIONSHIP

The "Game of the Year" in 1968 was with the Auburn Tigers. With us having only the tie against Tennessee in conference play and Auburn unbeaten in the league, the Southeastern Conference Championship was on the line at the "loveliest village on the plains." This was many years before the SEC split into two divisions and played a conference championship game at the Georgia Dome following the end of the regular season.

While we were 6-0-2 overall and unbeaten at 4-0-1 in SEC play, Auburn was good as usual and came into the game 6-2 overall. Their two narrow losses came in the season opener against SMU and against Georgia Tech, which had left the SEC after the 1963 season. The Tigers were a perfect 5-0 in conference games and could clinch the title with a win over us no matter how they did against rival Alabama the following week since the Tide already had two conference losses. Prior to the Auburn game it was the popular opinion that the winner would go to the Orange Bowl and play powerhouse Nebraska. We had an uneventful Southern DC-9 flight to Auburn, Al. and prepared for the big one.

The outcome of the game had huge implications: an SEC Championship for sure and a possible trip to the Orange Bowl. I recall Bill Stanfill, Billy Payne, Tommy Lyons, Brad Johnson, Bruce Kemp, Steve Greer, and some other players stepping forward before the game at a time when the coaches were not present and making statements on what the game meant to our families, fans, and school. It came from the heart.

The game was a typical Georgia-Auburn conflict, very physical and some frequent pushing and outright fighting. The two teams were similar in so many ways.

We had a slim lead going into the fourth quarter. After we scored, I will never forget the play made by Ken Shaw on the ensuing kickoff that was a major factor in allowing us to keep the momentum. Although Ken was a great high school player who had good speed and athletic ability, he was overlooked for a starting position because of the tremendous depth we had as a team. But he could really cover kicks and make tackles.

Ken was lined up on the far outside right next to me on the kickoff. Someone lost his lane in the middle, and the Auburn return guy popped it clean and was gone... I thought. I could not catch him, but Ken raced over from the opposite side of the field at an angle and pulled him down on about the 12 yard line. Our defense held them to a field goal, and they could never mount another threat as we won 17-3. That play by Ken made the difference in the game and eventually in our season.

I can recall the fans throwing oranges at us as we celebrated winning the SEC championship on the field after the game. The celebration was like nothing I had ever seen. It was awesome, a special moment of complete exhilaration for me.

However, little did we know as we celebrated on the return trip to Athens what was going to happen when we reported for film review the following Monday afternoon. The crap was about to hit the fan.

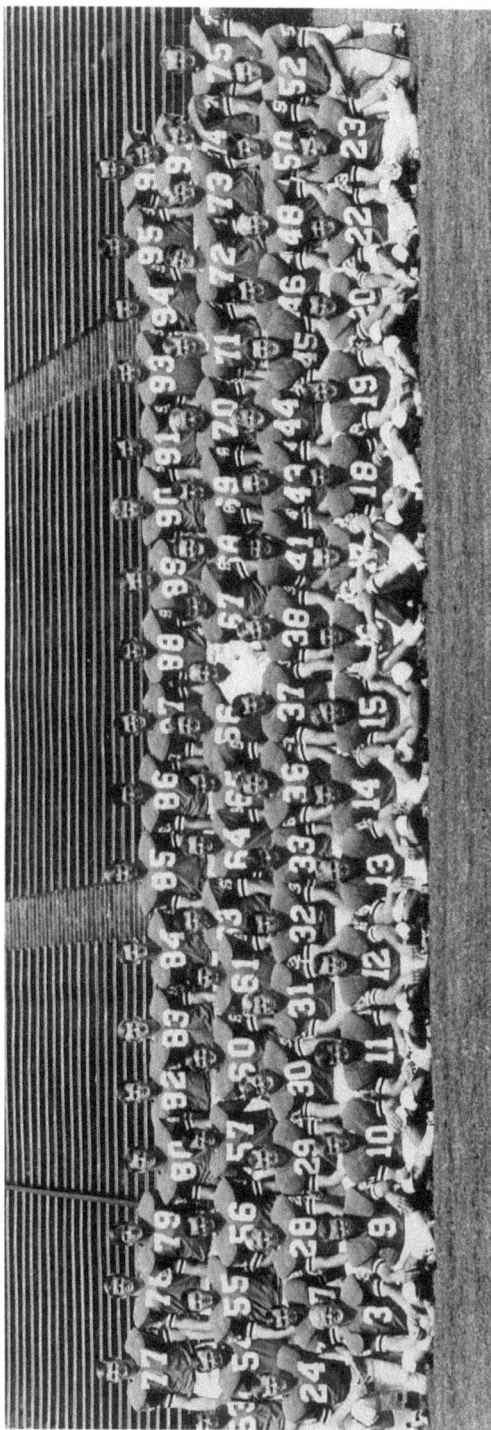

THE 1968 GEORGIA BULLDOGS – SOUTHEASTERN CONFERENCE CHAMPIONS

First row, left to right: Peter Rajecki, Bob Chandler, Paul Gilbert, Spike Jones, Mike Cavan, Jake Scott, Jack Montgomery, Glenn Davis, John Griffin, Donnie Hampton, Don Graham, Mark Stewart, Julian Smiley, Ed Allen, David McKnight.

Second row, left to right: Kent Lawerence, Penny Pennington, Bill Darby, Buck Swindle, Bruce Kemp, Trav Paine, Steve Woodward, Barry Outlar, Jim McCullough, Craig Elrod, Jimmy Shirer, Brad Johnson, Ronnie Huggins, Kerry Teel, Rusty Epperson, Steve Farnsworth, Bob DuPriest, Tommy Lyons, Jeff McKibben.

Third row, left to right: Tommy Couch, Mike Lopatka, Harold Tarrer, Geroge White, Happy Smith, Coach Vince Dooley, Jimmy Wood, John Jennings, Tim Callaway, David Rholetter, David Saye, Ronnie Rogers, Dennis Watson, Curtis McGill, Woody Woodall.

Fourth row, left to right: Bill Stanfill, Wayne Byrd, Buck Baker, Dennis Hughes, Lee Daniel, Sandy Johnson, Ken Shaw, Billy Brice, Mike Greene, Billy Payne, Phillip Russell, Charles Whittemore, Grig Herlong, Dennard Robison, Mayo Tucker, Terry Osbolt, Joe Clamon, Larry Brasher, Steve Brown.

THE ORANGE THAT TASTED LIKE SUGAR

I will make a key point here. The national rankings at that time were determined by the Associated Press and United Press International polls at the end of the regular season. With only seven or eight bowl games at the time, the outcome of those postseason contests had no effect on the final national rankings.

The competition was fierce among the bowls, schools, and coaches. Everyone was put in a difficult position to make key decisions that had huge financial implications which were predominantly for the benefit of the bowl sponsors, the school's athletic programs, and the school coffers. It was all about the money, and, unfortunately, the wishes of the players were often a secondary consideration.

With an off-week prior to the final game of the regular season against Georgia Tech in Athens, we were in the team film room at the Coliseum as usual on Monday. To our surprise, we were greeted by a group of public relations personnel from the city of New Orleans. They politely shook each player's hand as we entered the film room. I noticed a large reel of film on the projector that had been set up in advance of the meeting. Everybody looked around, and we were all kind of wondering what was up.

The PR guys from the Big Easy, dressed to the "nines," were seated on the front row. Coach Dooley took the stage and began to explain that the Sugar Bowl had offered our team an opportunity to play in their game on New Year's Day in New Orleans. He introduced the visitors, and they proceeded to show a lengthy film on all that was good about New Orleans and the Sugar Bowl. It was a full blown "hot box" sales pitch.

Very honestly, I was impressed with the presentation and thought playing in the Sugar Bowl would be great. But I also appreciated being part of a team that had just won a SEC championship and had an opportunity to play in a major bowl game.

Although most everyone on the team had been looking forward to playing in Miami's Orange Bowl if we won the SEC, the Sugar Bowl was fantastic to me. But I held my opinion to myself because it did not take a rocket scientist to know that my opinion did not represent the consensus, especially among the seniors.

Following the presentation by the New Orleans people, I was not privy to the meetings that the seniors held —with Jake included, of course— regarding the decision that Coach Dooley had made. But it was clear that there was resentment, disappointment, and outright anger. The majority

Members of the 1968 SEC Champion coaching staff, from left to right: Frank Inman, Doc Ayers, Jim Pyburn, Dick Wood, Ken Cooper, Erk Russell, Billy Kinard, John Donaldson, and Coach Vince Dooley. PHOTO PROVIDED BY THE UNIVERSITY OF GEORGIA DEPARTMENT OF SPORTS COMMUNICATIONS

of the team wanted to go to Miami and play in the Orange Bowl. Plain and simple, that opportunity was now gone without the players having any input or vote, as far as I knew. I must say that was the way it appeared. I have no knowledge if any seniors or team leaders were consulted prior to the Sugar Bowl decision. It was a mess.

The bowl situation simmered during the two weeks prior to the last game of the regular season. We had to focus on getting ready for the all important State Championship game: Georgia vs. Georgia Tech.

I played most of the second half for Jake as we beat Tech easily, 47-8. One special memory from that game was playing against Yellow Jacket quarterback, Kim King, who is regarded as a Tech legend. Unfortunately, Kim died of cancer a few years ago, but before his passing I had the opportunity to meet him again at Sea Island. Kim did the color on Tech radio broadcasts for many years and did a great deal for the Atlanta community during his life.

Another Tech player for whom I had a great deal of respect was Mike Wysong. Mike played slot receiver during the 1969-70 seasons with quarterback Eddie McAshan, Tech's first African American football player. Fast as lightning and very quick, he always smiled, liked to chat and had fun during games. I covered him one-on-one several times, especially when they realized that I was not a Billy Darby when it came to man coverage. The last time I talked to Mike was in the serving line at the Old Plantation Supper excursion to the south end of Sea Island, Ga. Unfortunately, one day several years ago I noticed in the AJC an obituary for Mike Wysong. He also died of cancer at a much too young age.

SENIORS VOTE TO BOYCOTT THE SUGAR BOWL

With the regular season completed with an unbeaten record of 8-0-2, the plot thickened with the Sugar Bowl situation. Meetings were held in confidence among the players, especially the seniors. There was outright resentment that the team leaders and seniors had not been consulted regarding the decision to accept the Sugar Bowl invitation.

Finally, the seniors voted to boycott the game! Yep, just refuse to play! Who in the world would have done that? I have never known of a college team ranked in the Top Five in the nation refusing to play in a major bowl game. But that was the position the seniors took, and they made it clear to Coach Dooley.

Although I understood the seniors' decision, I still wanted the trip and opportunity to play in a major bowl game very badly. I just nodded and bit my lip.

Negotiations began, and it was like the AFL-CIO and a Fortune 500 company during a strike. For days many issues were discussed between the coaches and the senior players. With the long break between the end of the regular season and New Year's, there was no practice for a few weeks. The underclassmen on the team just hung around waiting for something to happen. All was quiet for days, and no one was saying anything.

We were then notified that there would be a team meeting without any coaches present. The team leaders explained the financial magnitude of the game to the University and athletic department and went down a long list of reasons why the decision was made to accept the Sugar Bowl bid.

A list of "concessions," for the lack of a better term, regarding the players was presented. First, and the most significant as I recall, each player would be allowed the option to cash in his plane ticket and provide his own transportation to New Orleans as long as he reported at the appointed time. That was huge, and I believe, without exception, that option was exercised by every player.

There were other concessions regarding curfew times, certain days without curfew, extension of the length of the trip, I believe, from the original four days to seven, and some other concessions which I do not recall in detail. The team voted to accept the concessions offered and play in the 1968 Sugar Bowl.

Personally, I was one happy camper, but the team in general and especially several team leaders really could not forget what had happened. I believe that what transpired had a definite effect on the final score of our game against Arkansas in New Orleans on January 1, 1969.

THE BIG EASY AND THE SUGAR BOWL

I took my Delta Airlines ticket and along with a carload of players headed to Atlanta Airport and the nearest Delta counter to cash it in for just over $500, as I remember. It was a fortune to me, since the $10 per month laundry allowance just did not make it far, even in those days. The day after Christmas, I drove to Columbus, Ga. and met Penny Pennington and Bruce Kemp. With coolers packed and a few clothes, we took off for The Big Easy.

We arrived in New Orleans and immediately looked for Bourbon Street, particularly a place called Pat O'Brien's. The PR guys had told us how great it was, as well as Brennan's and many other really awesome restaurants. We visited Pat O'Brien's and enjoyed the "Hurricane," the traditional house drink served in a special signature class. The drink was designed to be a sipping beverage, but we kind of accelerated the process, much like "sipping" Old Milwaukee at a Seagraves Party.

Following our visit to Pat O'Brien's, we proceeded to the Fontainebleau Hotel in downtown New Orleans, a magnificent place. It was the first time that I had ever seen a real suite. I roomed with Mark "Craze" Stewart, who had already checked in.

The next few days included practice and some time on the town. We had no curfew for the first three days, and most of us took full advantage of the freedom. Bourbon Street was always alive, and the jazz music, which most of us had never heard live, was really good. We had a great dinner at Brennan's and when the flaming Bananas Foster was served I think one of our guys thought the house was on fire and took an early exit. Actually, it was a "first" for most of us. No doubt we made the most of the liberal curfew schedule, and the party was on.

Practice was the usual routine as we prepared for the Arkansas

Razorbacks, who won the Southwest Conference title that season. We went into the game thinking that we would beat them with no problem.

However, while we were enjoying a few days visiting Bourbon Street and other sites, the Arkansas team did not arrive in New Orleans until the day before the Sugar Bowl because they were going through two-a-days on campus in Fayetteville. In addition to being fine-tuned, they had a great passing combo in Bill Montgomery at quarterback and Chuck Dycus at receiver.

By the time kickoff for the Sugar Bowl arrived I frankly don't think we were the same team that posted an undefeated regular season and won the SEC title. The final rankings had been released, and we finished fourth in the nation. The bowl games at that time were only a financial and personal reward for the participants, but they were prestigious due the relative small number of bowls as compared to current times.

Everybody had enough of The Big Easy by game day, and our performance was indicative of the mood. Arkansas was ready to play and was well coached by Frank Broyles, who was destined for the College Football Hall of Fame.

Jake had a tough time covering Dycus. It seemed like every time we got in man coverage they would run an illegal pick play in the middle of the field. We screamed in protest, but to no avail. Our only score was a safety as we lost 16-2, our only defeat of the 1968 season in which we finished 8-1-2.

Penny, Bruce, and I loaded up after the game and headed back to Georgia. Overall, it was a great trip and a lesson in life learned by many.

OUTSTANDING INDIVIDUAL ACCOMPLISHMENTS DURING '68

Having an undefeated regular season and winning the Southeastern Conference Championship were great team accomplishments, but there were many outstanding individual performances. The 1968 season was a great year for our quarterback, Mike Cavan. Mike, a true sophomore, was named Sophomore of the Year and All-SEC. He had a great offensive line, and our fullback, Brad Johnson, was the best blocking fullback on the planet. We ran a sprint roll offense, and Brad knocked out defensive ends and outside linebackers like bowling pins.

Wingback Bruce Kemp played hurt most of the time, but was big and very fast for his size. Charles Whittemore, Kent Lawrence, and Dennis Hughes were steady receivers. The offensive line was anchored by Tommy

Lyons, David Rholetter, Pat Rodriquez, and Bruce Yawn who were solid and very consistent.

The '68 defense was lightning quick. Ronnie Huggins and Happy Dicks were outstanding linebackers. And yes, the tale of Lewis Grizzard writing a headline in the *Athens Banner-Herald* during the week prior to the Ole Miss game was true. Happy had been injured in the previous game and the headline read "Georgia plays Ole Miss with Dicks out." True story. Only Lewis could get away with that.

Tim Callaway, Steve Greer, Terry Osbolt, David McKnight, Lee Daniel, and Outland Trophy and consensus All-American Bill Stanfill comprised the Split 60 front. Coach Russell, our defensive coordinator and assistant head coach, said Steve Greer was the only defensive lineman he ever saw who could run around blocks consistently and make All-American. He was that quick. Greer could have been competitive as a cornerback.

Senior defensive tackle Bill Stanfill was a man among boys. A tremendous high school player in Cairo, Ga. Bill had all the tools to be a great strong side tackle in our wide tackle defensive scheme. At 6-6, 265 he was considered huge at that time, but of more importance were his range and speed, 4.6 in the 40 and arms like south Georgia oak branches. Bill made All-American, was named Outland Trophy winner as the nation's most outstanding interior lineman, and was drafted by the Miami Dolphins where he had an All-Pro career. He was a stalwart on the Dolphins' 1972 team that turned in the first and to date only undefeated record.

Rounding out the starting defense were Penny Pennington and Mark "Craze" Stewart, our starting cornerbacks, and Jake Scott, who was and remains the best safety in UGA football history. Penny was compact and quick and a rugged tackler. As for Craze, he was a real nut and invented trash-talking. Fast for his size at 6-2, he was a fifth year guy. Had it not been for Coach Russell and a few promises, Craze would not have come back for his final season. He was full of life and confidence and never had a bad day. On a personal note, I'll always be grateful to Craze for working behind the scenes to encourage the coaches to put me on scholarship. Craze and I remained in touch and were very good friends until he developed a tumor and died in 2008. Craze was a great guy, and I miss him.

As for Jake Scott, he was spectacular. I have never seen a more gifted athlete. A native of Greenwood, SC, he lived on zone anticipation and had a knack for outguessing opposing quarterbacks and reacting. Although he really did not watch film a great deal, Jake seemed to know what plays were about to develop. Blessed with excellent speed and stunning as a punt returner he was a big believer in balance drills and was rarely taken down by the first or second tackler on returns.

His name can be found throughout the Bulldog record book, including the most career interceptions and the most interception return yards in school history.

Although Jake had a year of eligibility remaining, he decided to turn pro after his junior season in 1968 and signed with British Columbia of the Canadian Football League, since the NFL at that time would only draft players who had completed their college eligibility. A year later he was drafted by the Miami Dolphins, where he joined UGA teammate Bill Stanfill. He was named Super Bowl MVP on the unbeaten Miami team of 1972 and was inducted in the State of Georgia Sports Hall of Fame in the mid-eighties.

HEADS UP #9

Always seek the absolute truth.

• Not all consensus is truth.

• Conditioning can be dangerous. Beware of following the crowd going the wrong way.

• Clear the emotion. Seek wisdom. Look for the facts, and the truth will prevail.

These are the things you are to do: Speak the truth to each other and render true and sound judgment in your courts.

– Zechariah 8:16

As noted earlier, I owe Jake a great debt of gratitude for agreeing to help me learn the safety position, turn my spring practice performance totally around which helped me earn a scholarship, and mentor me during our one and only season together.

The year 1968 was a memorable period in my life. From the misery of winter workouts in March, to packing my bags and coming within a few hours of transferring to Florida State prior to spring break, to almost quitting the team two weeks into spring practice, to signing a full scholarship with UGA, to being a member of the SEC Championship team, and finally to playing in the Sugar Bowl--- it was some kind of ride!

Coach Dooley has probably replayed the circumstances surrounding the 1968 season and the Sugar Bowl decision a few times over. I do not know if he would have made a different decision if he had it to do over, but my guess is he probably would have. To fully understand all sides one must understand that the bowl selection process was much different then than it is now. There was no BCS with computers playing a major role in the decision. Back in the day it was all about negotiating skills, timing, and serious deal making.

All the bowls were competing with each other and all the coaches were competing with each other. It was a pressure packed environment with a lot of money and prestige at stake. I am sure that Coach Dooley thought he was making the best decision at the time. It was kind of a "bird in the hand" concept, and it assured us of going to one of the top bowls, regardless of the outcome of the Auburn game.

It is an established fact that Coach Dooley turned Georgia Football around when he came to Athens in 1964 and in the years that followed when he built a national powerhouse. Coach Dooley was head coach at UGA for 25 seasons, averaged eight wins per year, accumulated 210 overall victories, and won six SEC Championships and one National Championship in 1980. He received SEC Coach of the Year honors in 1966, 1968, 1976, and in 1980 and was named the Bobby Dodd National Coach of the Year Award in 1976. He was inducted in the Georgia Football Hall of Fame in 1978 and the College Football Hall of Fame in 1994.

Additionally, Coach Dooley received the Eddie Robinson Coach of the Year Award and The Sporting News Coach of the Year Award in 1980. He later received the Walter Camp Award and the Amoz Alonzo Stagg Award in 2001, the Carl Maddox Award in 2004, the Homer Rice Award in 2007, and the "Bear" Bryant Award in 2010. Coach Dooley was also inducted into the prestigious UGA Circle of Honor in 2004.

Coach Dooley's record speaks for itself. I want to thank him for allowing me to share that Saturday night Bulldog feeling.

1969- THE SEASON I BECAME A STARTER

With the SEC title and trip to the Sugar Bowl now past history, life quickly got back to normal as we started classes for the 1969 winter quarter. Soon thereafter, the focus was on the '69 Bulldog edition as winter workouts in the weight room with Coach Sam Myrvos room kicked off.

I had resigned myself to being a backup up again since it was assumed that Jake Scott would be back for his senior season. My season as the starting safety would be a year away. Or so I thought at the time.

It was sometime in the middle of the night during early spring quarter

I was fortunate to letter 3 years, start 22 consecutive games, play on an SEC Championship team and meet many great people during my UGA years.
PHOTO PROVIDED BY THE UNIVERSITY OF GEORGIA DEPARTMENT OF SPORTS COMMUNICATIONS

when I was awakened by a loud thunder that sounded like a glass pack on a hot rod. The noise got louder and louder as it approached my door at McWhorter Hall. Jake had driven one of his super bikes up the front stairs of McWhorter Hall and right up to our room and revved up the motor to deafening levels. I was rooming with Mike Cavan at the time.

Jake banged on the door. "It's party time!" he screamed while waving a check for a considerable amount of money in his hand. He was ready to celebrate.

Mike and I didn't immediately ask any questions, but still half asleep we dressed and loaded up the car for a trip to the Brave-Falcon night club in Atlanta, Jake's favorite spot owned by ex-Bulldog and NFL player, Pete Case.

I was not sure what was going on, but as we began to come out of our stupor on the way to Atlanta, Jake showed us a contract that he had signed to play football for the British Columbia Lions of the Canadian Football League. It was a large amount of money.

Jake looked at me and said, "The job here is yours now. So go get it.

This was for me, but I had you in mind."

The night in Atlanta felt as if we had spent a month at the Brave-Falcon. We made it back to Athens sometime the next morning. Mike and I were the first to know that Jake had turned pro, but by mid-day it was national news.

SPRING BREAK 1969 – FRITZIE CLARK SAVED MY LIFE

I might as well get the other "guilt by association" story off my chest at this point. This was an incident that was much more serious than the time three years before when I was the unknowing get-away driver for some friends who "decorated" some trash cans at Berrien County High the week of our graduation. This one could have ruined my life and led to prison. It was serious business.

It was spring break at UGA. We had just won the SEC Championship, and everyone thought it was just the beginning of great things. Spring football practice, 28 days in pads concluded by the Red-Black game on G-Day, was scheduled to start immediately after spring break. But now, with classes and strenuous winter workouts completed, it was time to have some fun in the sun.

I invited two football buddies to go with me to Orlando to visit my biological father, Harry Clark, and his wife, Fritzie. It was amazing that although he was no longer my legal father, since I had been adopted by Papa James and changed my name to Swindle, we remained good friends. Papa Clark, as he is affectionately known within family circles, is a great person with whom I have a great relationship to this day. He is 93 and doing great.

The three of us made the long trip to Papa Clark's home in Kissimmee outside Orlando. We got in during the wee hours of the morning, cooked some steaks, and had a blast from the time we arrived.

We slept in a bit and later checked into our hotel. Later that night we met some locals we knew and were invited to a party at an apartment complex. It was a "happenin" party. We hung out with the locals for a while, but some things that were going on in the unseen areas just did not seem right to me so we decided to go back to the room.

It was about 1:30 a.m., and I was driving my Olds powder blue 442. I had been "responsible" and was ok to drive. As we backed out of the parking lot we noticed someone rolling on the ground in what looked to be excruciating pain. It was a young man about our age who we recalled seeing at the party. He was screaming and holding his leg. Someone had hit him in the parking lot, but we had no clue who the assailant was or where he came from.

With rain coming down, he came to my window and said he needed help. I told him to get in and we would drive him to the emergency room. He said there was no need to go to the emergency room, because he had a key to the "training room." All he needed was to get some ice and a brace for his leg.

I asked him where the "training room" was, and he gave me the directions. We pulled into a really nice parking lot beside what looked like a new Gold's Gym. Wrong: it was the spring training facility for one of the top major league franchises.

The guy hobbled up to the front door and inserted the key. We walked in like the manager would.

I could not believe it. Every locker was perfect. Jerseys with names of players most people would recognize today were neatly placed on wooden hooks. Game gloves and bats were polished to perfection and ready to head north for opening day in just a few days.

The kid immediately got into the whirlpool and later got an ice wrap and brace. He said he was a minor leaguer in AAA and had a real chance to make the team, but had a leg injury. He said the team trainer had given him a key so he could rehab on his own schedule.

We stayed in the training room with him about 45 minutes. He finished his whirlpool-ice routine, and we locked up and departed. After dropping him off at a nearby hotel he thanked us, and we headed back to our hotel. By three a.m. the lights were out. I had no clue what had happened while I was helping and talking to this young man.

After a few more days in Florida, we returned to Athens on a Sunday night, and I checked my mail box at McWhorter Hall as usual. There was a hand written note from Coach Dooley which instructed me to meet him in his office at 9 a.m. on Monday. I had a sudden blood rush and, needless to say, did not sleep well that night.

When I entered Coach Dooley's office the next morning I was not asked to sit so I stood. Coach Dooley proceeded to explain to me that the University of Georgia had been served with a criminal warrant for theft by taking, and my name was at the top of the list. The warrant was from the attorney representing both the major league team whose facility we had visited and a future Hall of Fame player.

I was in a state of shock. I had no chance for rebuttal or comment. Coach Dooley, a man of few words then and now, said to me, "You have come so far, but now it's all going down for us all. You have no idea of the implications of this incident to this institution."

Coach Dooley said he was not concerned about the circumstances. He wanted the jerseys, gloves and any other "stolen articles" returned or we would be facing law suits and embarrassment beyond our wildest dreams.

No doubt this was a "major league" challenge. I was in a funk of a lifetime for most of the week that followed, but we got things under control by Friday. My stepmother, Fritzie Clark, who lived in Orlando, was an angel. Somehow, after an extensive series of calls, she was able to locate the glove that had been stolen from the locker room. One of our guys had taken the glove from the locker room that night and had sold it for $30. I still don't know how she did it, but Fritzie somehow discovered who bought the glove. It was amazing!

All of the missing jerseys, shirts, and especially the glove showed up at the UGA Athletic Office on Monday morning, a week to the day

HEADS UP #10

You will become like your personal choices of association.

• Recognize the "Drain People" in your life. There are more than you think.

• Avoid the complainers, doomsayers, gossipers, whiners, and bullies.

• If you are in charge, take charge and do the right thing.

• No excuses: if you see it's wrong, avoid it and move on.

• Get energized with the motivators, dreamers, and workers.

• Outwork the competition. Work smart!

"Therefore, let all of Israel be assured of this God had made this Jesus, whom you crucified both Lord and Christ." When the people heard this, they cut to the heart and said to Peter and the other apostles, "Brothers, what can we do?" Peter replied, "Repent and be baptized, every one of you, in the name of Jesus Christ for the forgiveness of sins. And you will receive the gift of the Holy Spirit."

– Acts 2:36-38

when I was called on the carpet in Coach Dooley's office. We met and forwarded all the articles to the address listed by the attorneys. It was Wednesday when we received a call in which we were notified that all pending charges had been dropped against UGA by the star player and his major league team and written confirmation was in process.

I called Fritzie, and we talked for hours. Absolutely amazing! How she was able to put all the pieces together, especially in such a short time, is beyond me to this day.

Several years later at her funeral I once again thanked Fritzie for finding the glove and for the many other things that she did for me and my family during her lifetime.

SPRING PRACTICE 1969

Prior to the infamous spring break trip to Orlando, I was listed as the number one safety on the depth chart as I replaced Jake Scott who had turned pro. However, following the spring break incident my status changed dramatically from number one to the bottom at number five. You think who you hang with doesn't matter? Think again!

When we dressed for the first spring practice session, it was like I was back at the beginning: a no-name. By the end of the day I had spoken to most of my teammates and made a covenant with them that I would never let them down again.

Although several things changed in my life that day, I still wish that I had had a strong Christian commitment to go along with my promise. But it was all about me and my screw-up. At the time, Christ was still not in the picture.

I began spring practice as focused as I have ever been in my life. I lined up behind four other guys who had the opportunity to take "Jake's position." I can't remember Coach Dooley speaking to me during the entire spring. One thing was for sure though: I was going to do whatever it took to get back to the top of the depth chart. Jake's position was going to be mine by the time we kicked off in September.

At that point I had a "take no prisoners" attitude. I even got better at run support. Jake had taught me how to get to the deep outside, but he liked run support as much as I disliked it. Regardless, I was in a situation much like my first spring practice as a walk-on. I was never more dedicated than during the spring of 1969, but, once again, it was all about me. Christ would have been a great partner, but I was too busy with other things.

Coach Billy Kinard was my secondary coach at UGA during my freshman, sophomore, and junior years. He was from the old school, and if you saw the movie Junction Boys that highlighted Coach Bear Bryant's early years, you will know what I mean.

Coach Kinard loved the saying, "better lucky than good." He used it when you got a tipped pass for an "oskie" (football slang for interception), a receiver dropped a pass, or a quarterback overthrew a receiver who was wide open. I think what Coach Kinard really meant was that good luck comes as a by-product of hard work and dedication, much in the same way that faith comes as a byproduct of a strong Christian commitment. In my case, I was certainly luckier than good during most of my life experiences. My early career playing football was no exception.

There is no doubt that the episode in Florida during spring break made spring practice a special challenge. I had been given an opportunity of a lifetime when Jake went pro, and then I came within an eyelash of losing everything.

Keep it simple. Slow down and take care of the small things.

- Have a "Tech Day" off every two weeks.

- Read, meditate, and pray.

- Keep your goals simple, clearly defined, and written.

- Write a Personal Mission Statement and pin it to your wall to be in full view every day. Just do this. And no whining.

But when you fast, put oil on your head and wash your face, so that it will not be obvious to men that you are fasting, but only to your Father, who is unseen; and your Father who sees what is done in secret, will reward you."

– Matthew 6:17-18

Although I was demoted to the bottom of the depth chart, I kept battling and was doing well. I gradually worked my way back up the chart and by the end of the 28 day spring drills I was listed at number two. I started for the Black Team at free safety in the G-Day Game and had a good game. The number one safety, John Griffin, was moved to corner and after the spring game I once again was listed as the number one free safety. I was fortunate to start at safety for the next 21 consecutive games.

Following the conclusion of spring practice I was very relieved and confident. Not only had I returned to the number one free safety spot, but I was also listed as the number one punt returner. I had all summer to prepare myself to start for the UGA Bulldogs.

In order to get a jump on pre-season practice, I decided to attend summer school which would allow me to be on campus and work out on a regular basis with some of the other players. Spike Jones, our All-SEC punter, and I worked out every day. I probably caught over 500 punts that summer.

Summer school was great. Things were slower, and there were many opportunities to work out and hang by the pool in search of "co-educational advice." Summer school was really a "no brainer" when the alternatives were a tobacco patch and two 55-acre hay fields to tend.

GREAT EXPECTATIONS BUT LESS TALENT

We reported for fall practice in mid-August, and the expectations were high for the '69 Bulldogs. As the defending SEC Champions we were ranked pre-season number one in the conference.

However, we had lost a ton of quality players to graduation and Jake to professional football. Honestly, we just did not have the talent in numbers like the '68 team had.

Two-a-days were typically tough, especially for those guys who did not make the mile for time. Each player had been given a detailed day-by-day off season workout schedule without supervision. I discovered it was much easier to stay on the schedule at summer school than it was at home. The workout schedule prepared each player to run the mile for time at the beginning of two-a-days. Lineman and linebackers had a time of six minutes and thirty seconds. Time for the backs was six minutes flat. Spike and I ran together, and we both made our time for the second year in a row. We had a few starters, however, who did not make their times on the first day, and I think that kind of set the tone for our season.

My good linemen buddies, Ronnie Rogers and Jimmy Wood, made their times and provided leadership for our defensive interior.

I wasn't too nervous when we came out for the 1969 season opener against Tulane, a non-conference opponent, at Sanford Stadium. Bee had her trusty # 29 lunch box, and the season was under way.

We started out like gangbusters and won three straight over Tulane, Clemson and South Carolina. Two of the games were shutout routs, and we whipped the Gamecocks by 25. I was leading the conference in interceptions and punt returns. Spike was leading the SEC in punting and Bruce Kemp was the leading rusher.

However, in game four we hit a snag and lost by a TD against Ole Miss in Oxford. The "snag" was named Archie Manning. It was a memorable game for several reasons. Archie was in a league of his own as a player and was by far the best football player I ever played against. He was a Tim Tebow-type player before his time. If someone had placed Archie in the "Wildcat" shotgun type offense back then, he would have conquered the world.

There were many great quarterbacks in the conference at that time. Pat Sullivan was at Auburn, John Reaves at Florida, and Ken Stabler at Alabama were great players, but in my opinion none of them had Archie's athletic ability.

The Ole Miss contest was the only time that I can ever recall being totally physically exhausted after a game. It was about 100 degrees that day, and the Rebels had three sets of receivers that would alternate every three plays. Archie would spread them out and start scrambling. It was like playing against a no huddle offense. Even though we lost by only a touchdown, 25-17, Archie just wore us out that day in Jackson Memorial Stadium as our three-game winning streak to open the season was broken.

However, what happened a few hours after the game was far more memorable than losing the game.

With our heads down we boarded the two Southern D-C 9's in Jackson and were on our way to the airport in Atlanta. It became rainy and overcast as we got closer to the airport. I recall Bill Darby and I were playing gin, trying to get the game off our minds. I was sitting on the aisle seat with my tray table open. We all had seatbelts on as usual.

As our number one plane began its descent to land, it suddenly turned completely sideways, a 90-degree "adjustment" to the right in a split second. The cards and drinks were suddenly on the ceiling, and I almost hit my head on the floor of the plane. It was a mad house. Guys were screaming, and debris was all over the place. Several of the flight attendants who were not belted in had minor scrapes.

As the plane began a more gradual roll to the left to correct itself, we collected ourselves and began to pick up the mess. A flight attendant, who was white as a ghost, looked at me and just shook her head as if she was saying that she had no idea what had happened.

Following the landing we were told that our pilot made a "precautionary adjustment" due to an unauthorized private plane being in commercial air space. We later learned that our Southern DC-9 and the other plane were only 75 yards apart when our pilot made the "adjustment." I sometimes think about our near catastrophe, especially when I recall what happened outside Huntington, W. Va. the following year.

TOUGH SECOND HALF OF THE SEASON

Although we narrowly averted disaster on the return flight from Jackson, we were not as fortunate as far as the second half of the season was concerned. The balance of the year was tough.

We rebounded from the Ole Miss loss with two easy, high-scoring wins over Vandy and Kentucky and were 5-1. In the first six games we averaged over 30 ppg and allowed only 8 ppg. We had a solid defense that was ranked in the Top Ten in the nation and was statistically as good as the '68 team. However, little did we know, that we would not win another game following the victory over Kentucky in game six.

Things began to go the other way dramatically. We suddenly had difficulty scoring points and maintaining any substantial time of possession during the rest of the season. Tennessee surprised us with a 17-3 loss in which we were held to a field goal. That was followed by a disappointing 13-13 tie against Florida in Jacksonville when we missed an extra point that would have been the game-winner.

Individually, however, I was having a great year and continued to lead the Southeastern Conference in interceptions and punt returns. I had a real shot at Jake's single season SEC interception record of 10. I was two short with eight.

THE PLAY THAT CHANGED EVERYTHING

Now 5-2-1, we hosted Auburn in our eighth game on a cold, rainy day. I can remember rain freezing on our helmets and icicles hanging from our face masks. I could have used some gloves for my boney, freezing hands, but that was long before the advent of special gloves in football.

It was the second half, and although we were holding the Tigers on defense we could not muster any offense. As far as yardage gained Spike led the offense with some kind of record for roughing the kicker penalties, some of which were worthy of an Academy Award. The four or five penalties called against Auburn for roughing Spike kept us in the game.

Offensively, Auburn was also frustrated. The Tigers could not get their All-America receiver, Terry Beasley, open. Darby was like another layer of skin on Beasley, and Phil Sullivan, our other corner, was flip-flopping (when one specific defensive back is on a specific receiver) on Alvin

Bresler, the other talented Auburn wideout. I had a pick on Sullivan early, and our defense was GATA big time!

It was a typical third down and five yards to go at mid-field. According to our scouting report and defensive game plan this would be a sure passing down for Auburn. We called our normal split-man blitz with me taking the second inside receiver on the strong side which was # 80, the tight end. I tried to disguise the man coverage, but Sullivan looked me in the eyes and just smiled. The Tigers went against the plan, and Pat reversed and pitched it to tailback Mickey Zofko. Zofko had beady eyes, a buzz cut and was built like a box dump truck.

As Auburn pulled everything from the weak side but the kitchen sink, it looked like a stampede of blue and orange converging on the right corner. My #80 committed to a double team block with his left tackle so I had no doubt an all out sweep was in the making. I committed to support the run from the outside and met one of the Tiger "hogs" head on. I went low and stripped him down, but Zofko was headed north-south right behind his fallen teammate. Zofko hit me like a freight train. I can recall the crunching sound to this day. I rolled over and just sat on my all fours. The pain was so severe that I began to vomit down my jersey. I made it to the sidelines without losing a timeout.

Although I returned to the field after some medication, I gagged the rest of the game from the smell of vomit. I am physically reminded of that play every time I go the gym to this very day.

Our only score was a field goal, and we lost 16-3, the second time in three games that we had been held to a single field goal.

I was glad that my injury was not season ending, but it proved to be a constant, nagging and painful distraction. The balance of my playing days included membership in the "Needle Club." The routine of Cortisone on Thursday and Xylocaine three hours before kickoff allowed me to continue to play at the level that was expected of me and I expected of myself.

The season ended with a 6-0 loss to Tech in Atlanta when we only allowed six points on defense, but could not score. After scoring a grand total of two field goals in three of our last four games, we saw a season that started with so much promise end with a 5-4-1 regular season record.

I led the conference throughout the regular season in interceptions and punt returns until the last game when Bobby Majors of Tennessee had a career day against Vanderbilt and beat me by one pick and only a few yards in returns.

Surprisingly, despite the poor finish we were offered a bid to play Nebraska in the Sun Bowl. Nebraska was nationally ranked and went on to win two consecutive national championships in '72 and '73. Frankly, we had no business playing those guys. The trip to El Paso was great. Many of our guys had never seen cactus, and some of the "5 Star" establishments we found across the border in Juarez, Mexico were, shall we say, memorable. Since they said, "don't drink the water," we optioned for a cervesa (beer) substitute.

Actually, the trip to the Sun Bowl was more enjoyable in some ways than the Sugar Bowl trip the previous year, but the game was a nightmare. Although we were out-manned, we hung with the Huskers for a while defensively. I had two interceptions, and the team had four fumble recoveries, I believe. Nevertheless, we lost 45-6.

We were banged up pretty good after the game, and to make matters worse, Coach Kinard asked me to meet him at the bar in the hotel after the game. I thought that was a bit unusual since we were not exactly drinking buddies. Coach Kinard, who had been my coach from the day that Jake began to show interest in me, told me that he was going to Ole Miss to coach with his brother. I was devastated, but I understood. Mississippi was his home, and he had a great chance to move up to head coach, which he later did. He was very gracious during our talk and assured me that we would be fine. We had ended the season number one in the SEC in pass defense and had all three starters in the secondary returning for the 1970 season. We hugged like brothers, and I headed for Juarez with some teammates.

Since most of the liquor sales in Clarke County, Georgia at that time were done through "Trunk Show-Speakeasy" style bootlegging by aggressive frat guys, the demand for Tequila by most Bulldogs was not high. But that was not the case following the "taking to the woodshed" by the Huskers. I had my first and last Tequila Sunrise that night.

The five of us who made the short trip across the border came very close to missing the noon flight back to Athens. It was a long trip home. The 1969 season was in the books with a final record of 5-5-1. I made some All-SEC teams and was looking forward to my senior season.

UGA FOOTBALL: THE OFF-SEASON

There were many "interesting" activities that took place during my off-seasons at UGA, including a good weight and agility program headed up by Coach Sam Mrvos and Coach John Kasay. Coach Kasay was a former Bulldog player who had a "love affair" with the Sanford Stadium steps. He would often gather us at the Coliseum and set out to the visitor side of Sanford for an all out mini-marathon. Honestly, we had a blast! Coach Kasay would always lead the way. The father of veteran NFL kicker John Kasay, Jr., Coach Kasay recently returned to UGA as a part-time assistant strength and conditioning coach.

There has never been a more dedicated, well-conditioned Bulldog than Coach Mike Castronis, a three-time All-SEC Bulldog lineman during the mid-forties. Coach Mike was a "lead-by-example" kind of guy who often led many full court presses at age 73 during the regular pick-up basketball games at Stegman Hall. He could run with any 20-year old on campus—football player or not. Coach Mike was a team assistant under Coach Ayers and a great inspiration to all who had the pleasure to know him.

It is really difficult for the average person to know the level of commitment necessary to play football at the collegiate level. It was and remains today a year round process.

But when the season was over many players, including me, considered it time to have some fun. Everyone had their level of fun and sometimes academics got in the way of "extracurricular activities." The "fun" withstanding, however, the need to keep that GPA up and stay eligible was always lurking in the wings.

Living in the new, state-of-the-art athletic dorm, McWhorter Hall, we had regulations that were tough and were enforced by Coach Dick Copas. The rules really were not an issue during the playing season since everyone wanted to be at their best. But the off-season was a different matter. No doubt Coach Copas's enforcement was not as stringent during the off season, but he still had a job to do.

The rule that you had to eat breakfast every morning and sign in was a bummer. As I recall, if you missed three breakfasts in a month, you ran the Coliseum steps until you collapsed. Like most 20-year old kids, I was not the best housekeeper, but I got a wake up call during the 1969 off-season. I had been warned twice about not making my bed and missing one curfew, but I kind of blew it off until I was given an attitude adjustment, so to speak.

I was at home for a weekend, and good friend Rhett Dawson and some of the Florida State football jocks had a blowout party at Twin Lakes near the Florida line. We enjoyed the weekend so much that I decided to delay my return to Athens and drive back early Monday morning. I departed Twin Lakes around 1 a.m. and arrived in Athens about 5:30 a.m. I have had days that I felt better, for sure, so I planned to immediately hit the sack. However, I first checked my mailbox where I noticed a yellow slip of paper with some writing on it: "Due to excessive dorm rule violations you will meet me on the floor of the Coliseum at 6 a.m. Monday morning for some floor exercises—Coach Frank Inman."

You have got to be kidding me! I had partied most of the weekend, had not slept in 24 hours and had just gotten in from a five-hour drive from home. But now I had to hit the floor! It was like death, and I lasted for an hour and a half until I finally fed the fish, which I had the pleasure of cleaning up.

Coach Frank Inman was a great Christian man, as well as a fine and respected football coach. He was famous for his association with the Dye boys from Richmond Academy in their championship days. I had the pleasure of seeing Coach Inman during his later years when we visited Bee at the St. Simons Presbyterian Church, where Coach Inman attended.

No doubt, mornings like the one I spent with Coach Inman would get your attention, but we still tried to figure out ways to "end-run" the rules. There were cases of forging names on the breakfast list which took considerable practice in mastering someone's signature. It also took a considerable amount of rotation not to be recognized by Leonard Cobb, who was in charge of food service at McWhorter Hall.

The summers were great in Athens. The student body was half its normal size and most jocks were taking "routine" classes that were often make-ups for less than acceptable performance during the regular year. Some of the players considered summer school as penalty time, but it was like that rabbit in the briar patch as far as I was concerned. As I stated earlier my alternative to summer school in Athens was the hay field at Rolling Green Farm. It was a no-brainer, for sure.

It is amazing how creative one can be when necessity calls. I am sure if some of us had used the same creativity and imagination in our academics that we did in securing our vices the graduation rates would have been much higher.

SUBTERFUGE AT MCWHORTER HALL

One of the" Red Line" rules on the McWhorter Hall list of "don'ts" had to do with female visitation. It was clearly understood that female guests could only be admitted to the rooms on game day and had to be accompanied by parents. There were no exceptions. However, there was one particular player who lived in close proximity to me who developed a strategy to get around the female policy. This particular individual was well connected with certain co-eds at Rutherford Hall, an all-female dorm on Broad Street about a mile from McWhorter. The success of his strategy was based on timing and disguise. There was risk, but the rewards were worth the risk.

We knew the normal times for bed check, but on occasion Coach Copas would cross us up, which necessitated a little additional subterfuge. My associate had the ladies dress in guys' clothes and made sure that their ball caps did not show their long hair or pony tails. The girls came in pairs and made the mile walk from Rutherford to McWhorter and arrived at precisely 2 a.m. We had timed the walk, and all watches were synchronized.

The ladies made their way down the side of the steps and hid in the hedges; yes, McWhorter Hall had to have hedges too. The ready signal was three taps on the iron railing. The doors were unlocked for a ten-second entrance without a peep. It was done with the precision of a SEAL team exercise. We actually practiced the routine. Around 4 a.m., it was time for the exit strategy. For some reason, the exit time was not as exact as the entrance timetable. The exit was the exact reverse of the entry, and it always worked like a champ.

I recently spoke to the person responsible for our female visit strategy at McWhorter Hall. He retired a millionaire. I can understand why.

We also had an alcohol strategy at McWhorter Hall. Although the presence of beer or alcohol in the athletic dorm was strictly prohibited, it was quickly learned soon after the facility opened that a small compartment under the slats of each bed was a nice fit for a half-dozen Schlitz Malt Liquor Bulls.

It was always a challenge to find ways around the McWhorter rules, and eventually someone came up with the idea of the "secondary residence." I think it was suggested by one of the Rutherford Girls the day after she explained to us what she experienced when accidentally locking herself out of her room in the wee hours one morning. Three to four players would go in together and rent an apartment. We only used these facilities during the off season and for social occasions. My favorite "secondary residence" was located at Pickens Lake, a three-bedroom bachelor pad on a beautiful lake outside Athens. I shared the apartment with Bruce Kemp and Penny Pennington. It was an incredible setting, so nice that entire sororities would come out to grab some rays and hang out.

Then there were the trips to the nearby hamlet of Arcade, the beer capital of North Georgia. Clarke County, home of the University of Georgia, was a dry county at the time. However, Arcade, which was located in "wet" Jackson County about 15 miles up the Jefferson Highway, had at least four beer stores. The trips to and from Arcade were always an adventure. There aren't any Old Dogs from back in the day who do not remember the "Arcade Experience."

PI KAPPA ALPHA AND THE DOGS

There were several Pi Kappa Alpha brothers who played varsity football at UGA. My good friend from Valdosta, Glenn "Barnie" Davis, and Charlie Whittemore were my closest Pike-Dog connections. The Pikes seemed to be synonymous with athletics, both by having several varsity players as fraternity brothers and by being a dominant force in the various most intramural sports. We had many good times just hanging out at the Pike House.

As related earlier, I had plenty of opportunities to thank Mo Thrash, Barry Henry and Billy Ozier for their assistance in getting the "Modified American Plan" at the Pike House during the spring of 1968 when I found myself without a dorm room at UGA following my decision to abort the transfer to Florida State. I see Billy Ozier often since he is local to Carrollton and owns one of the best embroidery and screen-printing companies in our area, Ozier Products.

One of the most memorable experiences as a Pike took place in the spring of 1969. It was a typical spring Saturday afternoon in Athens. Spring practice was over, and we were chilling out on the front porch of the Pike House with some fraternity brothers and a cold keg. This particular day was special for one of our rival fraternities, Kappa Alpha, since they were celebrating their annual "Old South Ball." The KAs dressed up in Confederate dress grey uniforms with sabers, tackle twill, brass buttons— the works! Some of their guys would grow a beard for six months in an effort to look as much like a Confederate general as possible.

The uniforms looked authentic. It was serious business for those guys.

As the KA "rebels" assembled up the street above our fraternity house, we Pikes thought this annual "costume ball" by our rivals was a bit much. It looked like the 15th Alabama Regiment was about to make a charge up Little Round Top. The Confederates were soon joined by their Southern Belles dates who were dressed in hooped dresses and wide brim hats. All of them had Mint Juleps in hand.

Since our Pike House was only a few lots down from the KA House, there always seemed to be some "issues" going on between the PKA and KA brothers. We discovered some time later there was also a personal feud brewing between with one of the Pike brothers and the president of KA regarding a female. Our Pike brother was a hard core Georgia coastal boy from McIntosh County who was the type who could go to Sapelo Island with a backpack and a homemade long bow and not come back for a week.

As the KA-Confederate contingent began its march on the upper end of Lumpkin Street, we noticed that the KA president was leading the parade mounted on a beautiful Arabian horse with a long mane. We also noticed that our fraternity brother who was having the "disagreement" with the KA president had disappeared. As the parade leader on horseback passed in front of our fraternity house's porch, we heard a popping noise. At the instant we heard the pop, the beautiful Arabian horse began to hop on all fours like they were Pogo Sticks as Mr. KA hung on to his mount's mane for dear life. Horse and rider began a wild journey that finally ended at the Five Points intersection at least three miles away! Following an intense investigation, the cause of the horse's action was never officially determined nor was a perpetrator identified.

A few weeks after Kappa Alpha's Old South celebration, however, some of our Pike guys were hanging out over a Boston Butt cooking when our friend from McIntosh County asked us out of the blue, "Have any of you ever seen a pellet gun with a scope?"

He added with a knowing smile, "I have one."

Ahh, the "The Off Season" of UGA Football. Those were the days! The conditioning drills and spring practice withstanding, it was a short period of time when the intensity and seriousness of the playing season took a back seat to fun and relaxation.

1970- MY SENIOR SEASON

The 1970 college football season will always be remembered for the tragic event of November 19, 1970 when the Marshall University football team's plane crashed on a stormy Saturday night, just short of the Huntington, W. Va. Airport. There were no survivors.

The crash touched to varying degrees the lives of every young man who played the game, every man who coached the game, and every fan who cheered on Saturdays. Those of us who played and coached took the tragedy very personally. It was if a plane full of our brothers had been killed on that hillside. If you loved the game of college football from the field or from the stands, it rocked all of us.

As for the 1970 Georgia Bulldogs football team, it was much like its immediate predecessor. We returned a strong defense that included all three starters from the secondary, plus some really good new players like Chip Wisdom and Buzzy Rosenberg.

Secondary Coach Kinard was replaced by Coach Gary Wyant, who came to us from Florida State. Ironically, if I had gone to FSU as I had planned in the spring of 1968, Coach Wyant would have been my position coach there. Coach Wyant brought with him a new defensive secondary scheme. I never understood why such a radical change was made. After all, our secondary was ranked at the top of the SEC for the past two years, and we had all the guys back with Bill Darby and me as seniors.

As a detail oriented person, Coach Wyant assigned us tons of paperwork to learn under his new defensive system. We switched from a basic three-deep secondary with a lot of man on the corners and one free safety—me. Today, this scheme is known as Cover Two or zone corners with two safeties on each hash. The concept was complicated, and we were often thinking rather than reacting.

Our offense continued to struggle.

The 1970 season did not start on a good note, to say the least. We lost our season opener in New Orleans against Tulane by a field goal, 17-14, rebounded to shut out Clemson 38-0 at home, and then lost our first two conference games by a point against Mississippi State, 7-6, in Jackson and by 10, 31-21, at home against Ole Miss. Four games into the schedule we were 1-3 overall and 0-2 in the SEC. Not too good.

In the next three games, however, we seemed to turn things around with fairly impressive SEC wins against Vanderbilt and Kentucky and a blowout of South Carolina. We were now 4-3 and even in the conference at 2-2 going into game seven against the Gators. Maybe there was hope for a good season after all.

Jake had taught me that it was the safety's sole responsibility to get to the deep outside in the Split 60 scheme. I was very comfortable with that concept, and the proof was in our performance the previous two years. But when we were in Cover 2 I was always wondering what the other safety was going to do. I never had confidence in the scheme, but as a senior leader and preseason All-SEC candidate I did not complain until our return trip from Jacksonville and the game with Florida. I'll always remember the conversation with Coach Russell, our defensive coordinator, on the plane flight home.

Earlier that day we had played Florida on national television. With the scored tied at 17-17 the Gators had the ball just over midfield with about a minute to play. Their All-American receiver, Carlos Alvarez, was their go-to receiver, and he had hurt us all day with underneath hooks and slants. John Reaves was a pinpoint passer, and Carlos had some jets and hands like glue. It is amazing that with all the recent great Florida teams, Carlos still holds the all-time UF receiving record.

When the Gators came out in a wide slot with a split backfield I knew they had to go deep since time was running out. Carlos was the outside receiver to my right and the slot receiver was 10 yards inside. They ran a route that they had not run all day or all year for that matter, a double-post pattern in which both receivers ran posts to the middle.

I was playing safety on the left hash, and I moved just a step to my left as the slot guy cut. But in my heart I knew Carlos was the man. My instincts told me to move back to centerfield, but I was a fraction too late. I remember the ball touching the tips of my fingers as I extended to make a play. I hit the ground, rolled and watched Carlos cross the goal line.

Everybody told me, "It was not your man." But those comments brought little solace when I awoke the next morning and saw myself in a photo on the front page of the *Atlanta Journal-Constitution* as Alvarez crossed the goal line for the winning touchdown. It was not the front page of the sports section, but the front page of the entire newspaper! I have the clipping.

I was devastated during the flight home when Coach Russell called me up to his seat. He was not upset. He just wanted to know what I thought we should do to make the new system work. Although we had just played our eighth regular season game, the system was still "new" in many ways.

I suggested that we scrap it and go back to man-free coverage. Coach Russell said he would consider it, and I returned to my seat.

Looking back, I don't think most of the coaches involved believed it was worth the change so late in the season. I would find out at practice on Monday.

THE LEGENDARY COACH ERK RUSSELL

In regard to Coach Russell, this is a good time to make special mention of the truly special opportunity and privilege I had of playing for one of the finest coaches and gentlemen who ever set foot on the field of play. Coach Erskine Russell was the legendary, long-time defensive coordinator and master motivator of the Bulldogs during the '60s through the early '80s. He meant business and had a gift for being both an authoritarian and a friend.

> Coach Erskine Russell was the legendary, long-time defensive coordinator and master motivator of the Bulldogs during the '60s through the early '80s.

The originator of the storied nickname, "Junkyard Dogs" of the mid-'70s, Coach Russell also came up with the idea of the "TEAM – me" tee shirts that are still seen today. I'll also give him credit for the "GATA" penned on masking tape that was placed on our practice helmets. Initially, I was embarrassed for not knowing what the letters meant. I learned that Coach Russell re-arranged the letters of the Georgia Tech Athletic Association (GTAA) to spell "GATA," which meant "Get After Their Ass." We wore the "GATA" tape on our helmets in every practice session.

I have never forgotten what "GATA" means, and evidently neither has the football program at the University of Georgia. Nearly 40 years after Coach Russell coined the legendary acronym the following appeared in a November 29, 2010 column by *Atlanta Journal-Constitution* sports writer, Mark Bradley, in which he criticized the lack of an aggressive playing edge by the 2010 Bulldog edition:

> *An acronym born under Erk Russell is still written on the board before every Georgia game — GATA. (Loosely translated, "Get After Them Aggressively." The Bulldogs, however, have become slow learners. They didn't take a lead against an SEC opponent until the season's fourth conference game.*

Many of you longtime UGA fans and foes alike probably remember seeing Coach Russell on the sideline during games with a gash on his forehead and blood streaming down his face. During pregame warm-ups and sometimes during the games he would butt heads with his players to get their attention or single them out for making an exceptional play.

My good friend Ronnie Rogers was a standout down lineman during those years and experienced many of those bloody circle butt pre-game drills. Ronnie, like most players who played directly for "Erk," has a special place in his heart for that man, as do I.

I can recall the letters Coach Russell sent to all the defensive players during the summer in which he reminded us to "run three miles and hate Tech five times each day." I can't recall a starter on defense failing to make the designated time in the mile run that was part of the pre-season conditioning requirement.

One of Coach Russell's "summer letters" which I am proud to have in my possession was written several years after my final summer as a player at UGA. However, this one holds special significance since he sent it to the players during the summer prior to the Bulldogs' National Championship season in 1980. It can be found on the following page.

The tremendous success that Coach Russell enjoyed as assistant head coach and

The legendary Erk Russell was a player's coach and a player's best friend. His players would die for him if that is what it took. PHOTO PROVIDED BY THE UNIVERSITY OF GEORGIA DEPARTMENT OF SPORTS COMMUNICATIONS

defensive coordinator at UGA from 1964 to 1981 is clearly evident in the following numbers: in 192 games that he coached opponents scored less than 17 points in 135 of them and single digits in 74. I am proud to say that I played for Coach Russell in 29 of those games and started 21 of them during my three years of wearing the "GATA" label.

After leaving UGA following the 1981 season and taking on the challenge of starting football from scratch at Georgia Southern University,

department of athletics
p.o. box 1472

the university of georgia
athens, georgia 30613

July 7, 1980

Gentlemen: (and Linemen)

The football season of '80 will be my seventeenth as a Georgia Bulldog. During this time there have been many thrilling Saturdays of competition, each with it's individual memories, because each game has it's own personality.

There are two Saturday traditions and experiences which have remained basically the same throughout the years for me and I would like to share them with you.

The first one concerns THE RAILROAD TRACK CROWD. These are my people because they love the 'Dogs almost as much as I do. Oh, I know they do some crazy things - like turn over our opponent's busses sometimes and now and then they throw one another down the bank and into the street below. But they stamp out Kudzu and they pull for us to win and that ain't bad.

If you can get off the bus to the cheers of THE RAILROAD TRACK CROWD and walk down those steps to the dressing room and not be inspired to play football as best you possibly can, something important is missing beneath the Georgia jersey you wear. It is impossible not to be inspired. They choke me up!

The season of 1980 will be the last for THE RAILROAD TRACK CROWD. A great Georgia tradition will have passed with the new addition to our stadium. The view from the tracks will be no more.

Your team will be the last Georgia Team to be greeted and cheered by THE RAILROAD TRACK CROWD. Wouldn't it be fitting if their last team was also the best Georgia Team ever. Think about it!

Another Saturday tradition which has meant so much to me over the years can be stated very simply: "THERE AIN'T NOTHING LIKE BEING A BULLDOG ON SATURDAY NIGHT - - - - - AFTER WINNING A FOOTBALL GAME". I mean like whipping Tennessee's ass to start with, then ten more and then another one.

This is the Game Plan. We have no alternate plan.

Sincerely,

Coach Russell

Erskine Russell
Assistant Head Football Coach

ER:nn

P. S. Run!

AN EQUAL OPPORTUNITY/AFFIRMATIVE ACTION EMPLOYER

Coach Russell led his Eagle teams to three NCAA Division 1-AA National Championships and was coach of the first college team of the 20th century to go 15-0.

Coach Russell was named the Georgia Sports Hall of Fame Coach of the Year for 1984-86 and was inducted into the Georgia Sports Hall of Fame in 1987 and the Alabama Sports Hall of Fame in 1991. He was USA Today's Georgia Coach of the Year and for the decade in 1989. Also in 1989 he was selected as the Chevrolet-CBS Sports 1-AA Coach of the Year. In 1996 Coach Russell was a torch bearer for the Olympic Games.

But no matter what award or accolade he received, I am sure that Coach Russell received it with humility and appreciation. I am also sure that he would much prefer a session of breakfast and discussion at "Snookys," the fabled Statesboro restaurant owned by good friend and teammate, Bruce Yawn, than attending a tight-fitting formal awards ceremony.

In addition to being a remarkable coach and person on and off the field, Coach Russell had a great sense of humor. He would repeat the same corny and funny jokes like the one about it "taking 1,000 men to lay Virginia Pipillini," which Coach insisted was actually a misspelling by the commentator that should have read the "The Virginia Pipeline." He even made sure that we all knew where he bought his beer.

Coach Russell was a player's coach and a player's best friend. His players would die for him if that is what it took.

In 2006 at the age of 80, Coach Russell retired to God's plan for a Split Man Blitz. Many players and coaches attended Coach Russell's life celebration and teammate, Bruce Yawn, gave an eulogy for the ages.

Thanks, Coach, for "just one more time."

WHADDYAGOT LORAN?

There has never been a more dynamic duo is sports radio broadcast history than the team of Larry Munson and Loran Smith. Larry was the legendary "Voice of the Georgia Bulldogs" for 42 years. There is not a member of the Bulldog faithful who does not remember the call he made in the 1980 Georgia-Florida game with his "run, Lindsay, run." Larry Munson was amazing with his candor and emotional timing. He is forever missed on the radio airwaves, but remained active as an avid reader, book club leader, and movie-goer, until his death on November 20, 2011. Thanks for the years, Larry. We will never forget you!

Loran Smith served the UGA Athletic Department as a sideline

Loran Smith (left), longtime sideline reporter for the UGA football radio broadcasts, greeted Buck at the annual Lettermen's Reunion at the 2009 Kentucky game.

reporter on the radio broadcasts for 36 years, as well as serving in many other sports promotional roles. He also has been a successful author of several books associated with the Bulldogs. Although he has courageously and successfully fought a potentially life threatening illness, Loran has remained a loyal and dedicated Bulldog through the tenure of at least five UGA head football coaches. The Loran Smith Center for Cancer Support at Athens Regional Hospital, which offers information, education and emotional and spiritual support to cancer patients and their families in North Georgia, is named in his honor.

Loran continues to remain an active participant during the Georgia radio broadcasts with his famous "Tailgate Show" with co-host Neil Williamson.

Most fans are not aware of how much these two Georgia Bulldog icons, Larry Munson and Loran Smith, have done for former players and fans off the field of play and away from the microphones. I have seen this first hand, and I greatly appreciate my longtime association with them.

NOVEMBER 19, 1970

Following the loss against Florida, we played on the road the following week at Auburn. The Tigers came into the game 7-1 overall and 4-1 in the conference with their only loss being to Louisiana State by a touchdown. But following the setback to LSU, they routed Florida, 63-14, and Mississippi State, 56-0 and were on a roll going into our game. Pat Sullivan and Terry Beasley had a field day against the Gators. By comparative scores against the Gators we were a 57-point underdog, although the official spread had us as 23-point underdogs.

When we reported for practice on Monday to start preparing for Auburn, I noticed that Coach Wyant was not particularly conversant with me. I learned that Coach Russell had informed him that we were switching back to man-free in the Split 60 defense. Coach Wyant did not have much to say to me all week, and practice was not the greatest.

Few of us thought we had a chance at Auburn, but Coach Russell got us going later in the week. We had our old system back.

We knew Auburn was going to be cocky. The Tigers were nationally ranked coming into the game with us. Sure enough, they came out with the trash talk and swagger.

There was film of a blazing fire. I watched in amazement as the story of the crash of the Marshall University football team and staff unfolded. I was in shock.

Our offensive coaches took a chance in the Auburn game on a young kid at running back by the name of Ricky Lake. Ricky had not played much all year, but was very strong and had good speed. Against the Tigers, he had the game of his life in leading our offense. Defensively, we manned up on their outstanding receivers, Beasley and Bresler, and shut down Sullivan's air game. Auburn was never in the game, and their swagger had disappeared by the time we shook hands and walked off the field at Jordan-Hare Stadium with a shocking 31-17 upset. The date was November 19, 1970.

Although we flew to Auburn as a team, we were given the right to drive back to Athens with family or friends if we wished. We headed up I-85 and were excited. It was by far my best game all year, as well as the team's most outstanding performance.

My group of family and friends arrived in Atlanta at Warren Sewell,

Jr.'s home in Buckhead about seven p.m. Mr. Sewell was the uncle of Carol Worley, who I was dating. The TV was on in the kitchen, and I quickly noticed that every channel was carrying the same breaking-news item. There was film of a blazing fire. I watched in amazement as the story of the crash of the Marshall University football team and staff unfolded. I was in shock.

Bill "Red" Dawson, my good friend Rhett's older brother, was a coach for the Thundering Herd and was listed as being on the return flight from their game at East Carolina. I immediately called my mother, and she had already talked to Rhett's mother. From that time until around noon the next day everyone thought Red was on the plane. But as things turned out, he wasn't on the flight. As depicted in the

Rhett Dawson is a good friend I grew up with in the Ray City-Valdosta area. Rhett was an All-American receiver at Florida State and an NFL player with the Houston Oilers (pictured above) and the Minnesota Vikings. He autographed a picture to "Ole Boy," – his nickname for Papa James, and "Betty," – my mother, Bee. PHOTO COURTESY OF RHETT DAWSON

movie of a few years ago, "We Are Marshall," Red skipped the ill-fated flight at the last minute and drove from Greenville, North Carolina to Huntington, West Virginia. Other than the freshmen, some redshirts, and injured players who had not made the trip, Rhett's brother was the only surviving member of the entire Marshall football program. He was the only coach left.

November 19 was a great day on the field for the Georgia Bulldogs with our stunning upset victory at Auburn, but it was a horribly sad day for anyone associated with college athletics throughout the nation. Our euphoria quickly dissolved into shock and sadness. To say that things were suddenly put in perspective was an understatement. We were relieved to hear the news Rhett's brother had not been on the plane, but the impact of such a horrific accident was still difficult to imagine.

During the two weeks before hosting Georgia Tech in the final game of the season, we took advantage of the off-week, gradually adjusted, and prepared for the Yellow Jackets. The extra week off gave us some time to heal our bumps and bruises suffered during the previous nine games. My shoulder that had been injured during the game against Auburn the previous season held up as long as I stayed in the needle line. I had little pain during games. It was during the week when I had no medication that I had the most discomfort.

Tech came into the game with a new quarterback. Their star signal-caller, Eddie McAshan, was unable to play and Jack Williams got the call. Williams had a career day against us, and we lost the game 17-7 to finish the season 5-5-0. Obviously, no bowl invitation came our way.

I think every player remembers how it feels when he takes the pads off for the last time. I can still picture the final bus ride after the game from Sanford Stadium to the Coliseum.

As I wound down from the end of the season and my college football career, I gradually became upbeat and believed that I had an opportunity to be selected in the NFL draft. I had communications with several teams, but shortly after the end of my football career at the University of Georgia things began to unravel for me.

IV

THE DARK DAYS

I played my last football game ever on November 28, 1970 against Georgia Tech. With the exception of the nagging shoulder, I was in great physical condition when I left the field for the final time.

Having received inquiries from the Buffalo Bills, I thought I would be drafted by the Bills or another NFL team. I also had been talking to the Toronto Argonauts of the Canadian Football League and eventually signed a contract with Toronto rather than take a chance as a free agent with Buffalo. Toronto told me I would start, but Buffalo made no promises. I went with the Argos.

Jake Scott had told me that I was good enough to play in the NFL if I got stronger and had my shoulder rehabilitated. He was probably right, but I did not do the things necessary to make it happen. Forty years later I still don't know why things went so crazy with me during the 16 months that followed my last game as a Georgia Bulldog.

Somehow, some way for an extended period of time following my playing days at UGA, I became completely disconnected with reality. From December, 1970 to March, 1972 I developed a pattern of behavior that haunts me to this day in many ways. It was a period of time when I became heavily involved with gambling and pills.

I had enjoyed a game of Seven Card High-Low from time to time between football seasons at UGA, but it was no biggie, as my friend, Bull, would say.

When pulling an all-nighter "cram" before exams, I, like many students, took a pill or two. While the "Greenies" could be bought with a diet suppressant prescription, the extremely potent "Black Beauties" were strictly homemade.

Some of the guys figured out that a Greenie taken early in the morning of game day combined with a Black Beauty popped one hour before kickoff did the trick. I knew who followed this routine and stayed clear of those guys just before running out of the locker room to play.

I cannot imagine how many Black Beauties I took during the 16-month period after playing my final game. It's by the grace of God that I didn't take one that was contaminated with a lethal poison. There were several known cases of UGA students poisoned by contaminated pills. I'm sure most incidents were kept under the radar and never reported.

Taking Black Beauties on a regular basis had not been an issue with me until the those days following my final football game. I suppose I thought that since football was over it was my time to chill out, so to speak.

At the time I had no spiritual connection, and I had no commitment to finishing my degree. Although I had accumulated more than enough total hours needed to graduate, the course credits were all over the place. I was well short of the specific credits required to graduate with a degree in journalism. I had fallen to the temptation of taking "designated electives" just to make sure I remained eligible under the NCAA guidelines.

Certain courses such as geology, known to the jocks as "Rocks," and astrology, known as "Stars," were available to those of us who needed to boost their grade-point averages. It was amazing that we were encouraged to take these types of courses. I remember an instructor laughing and saying, "Okay, the offense sit on this side and the defense sit on the other."

If you could walk through the door and fog a mirror you could make an A.

There is but one person to blame for this lack of judgment, and that is me. There were many players who avoided the academic trap, pursued the correct curriculum, and earned their degree. That was a huge accomplishment, considering the responsibility and time commitment required to play college football while concurrently working toward a college degree.

I sacrificed a great opportunity to receive a college degree. I have paid for it the rest of my life.

MY FOCUS IN LIFE SHIFTED
FROM ONE GAME TO ANOTHER

I had no real, burning desire to play football anymore. Had I possessed the same resolve and purpose that I had when I walked on at UGA in 1967, I believe there is no doubt that I would have had a career in the NFL.

Two of the critical things that I lost during those early years following my college days were my dignity and sense of purpose. I slowly became associated with a group of people I should have never have known, much less become involved with.

I started a pattern of gambling on an almost nightly basis. I knew where every 7-Card High-Low game was being played from Athens to Atlanta. 7-Card High-Low was all I played, and I was good at it, especially late in the night when the pills were kicking in and others were drinking and becoming inattentive.

Playing poker was serious business with me. I could read my opponents around the table like a book, and I learned to count cards which helped me figure odds, especially near the end of each deck. I seldom drank during a game and when I did the pills, it seemed to overtake the feeling of a few beers. Some of the games that I played used four decks in a card shoe. Playing with four decks significantly increased the difficulty of card counting, but I worked out a system and was successful. Why didn't I use that same desire and innovation in those journalism courses and with a commitment to Jesus?

Eventually, I was able to leave behind the nightly, pill-fueled high stake poker games, and I have no desire to play any type of poker today. But I think it is meaningful to share the memory of one particular hand of poker that I had in a pro game in Athens.

I was only 20 years old and was in a game with the big boys from Atlanta late on a Tuesday night. 7-Card High-Low is a game played with each player receiving seven cards. The first two are dealt face down, and the next four are face up. The last card, or the "River" card, is face down. As the cards are dealt bets are made.

The game is a split-pot paid to the winner of the best high hand and the best low hand. Each player plays all seven cards to determine the best five-card hand from the seven cards dealt. It is possible, but rare, to have both the best high hand and the best low hand among the seven cards dealt. The best low hand is an ace, two, three, four, and five, and the same combination of cards is also a straight. In the game of 7-Card High-Low the combination can be used as a high hand as well. Holding this "swing hand," the player has the option to go either high, low or "swing" both ways. If the player chooses to "swing," he must win both ways. A swing is risky. If a tie occurs it is almost always a tie with another low hand. In this particular game, I thought it would be just one of many thousands of high-low hands in my years. I was wrong.

The pot was huge, and after the sixth card had been dealt I didn't have a combination of cards for either a high or low. I had the 2, 3, 5 and 6 of spades which was 4 to a low and 4 to a flush with the "River" card to be dealt.

Very honestly, I never even thought about the possibility of a straight flush. The bet was to me with maximum raises, and I believe a $120 call, a lot of money for a 20-year old kid. I thought seriously about folding since I only had $40 left after the $120 call. But for some reason I made the call, and I took the "River" card face down. I was afraid to look, and I put all three hole cards together and slid the new addition back very slowly.

Drugs kill.

- It only takes one bad decision to let drugs into your life. Some are instantly addictive.

- You never know if you can handle legal drugs and alcohol. Just because drugs are prescribed and are legal doesn't mean you should take them.

- Know that pharmacists are in business to sell drugs, and like every other profession, there are good ones and bad ones.

- Just because a drug like valium, oxycotin, and Demerol is prescribed and is legal does not make it any less addictive.

- We do not need as much "pain medication" as product advertisements claim.

Listen, my son, and be wise, and keep your heart on the right path. Do not join those who drink too much wine or gorge themselves on meat, for drunkards and gluttons become poor, and drowsiness clothes them in rags."

– Proverbs 23:19-21

I first noticed it was black. Good start to a possible flush if it was just any spade. I then slid the new card further and noticed it was a spade. Awesome, I first thought. I had a flush.

At first I did not notice that it was the 4 of spades! When I realized what I was holding it was like a hot branding iron hit me in the face. I lost my cool. I really think the guys thought I was creating a scene to support a bluff. I had caught the 4 of spades to make an inside straight flush, as well as a perfect low hand! By now, the pot was littered with 50's and 100's.

I regrouped and got under control. A couple of guys had what appeared to be high hands, and the betting increased. But my concern was losing a "swing" to another perfect low. I had lost my card count, and it was near the end of a single deck game.

The bets were maximum again. We always declared the high or low position verbally. The person making the last raise or bet was required to declare first. I never raised the bet. The other players bet my hand for me all the way, and I declared last.

There were four players who had stayed in the game. The first two players declared high, and the third declared low, which I had predicted. I took a deep breath and hoped the guy who had declared low was not perfect. I said in a faint voice, "I swing!"

There was complete silence for what seemed an eternity. I then turned over my hand that showed a nickel straight flush, and their mouths dropped. Also on the table was a heart flush and a queen full house for high, and the low hand was a 6-4 which was the next thing to a perfect low. I took the entire pot of over $3,000, and the night was never the same.

I wanted to leave after winning the huge pot, but the group "insisted" that I stay a bit longer. Although it was an hour before daylight, I had taken a second pill and was good to go. We played until about 11 a.m. the next day. I won a ton of money during that day-night session.

As the days passed and still riding the euphoria of that once-in-a-lifetime hand I lived to play High-Low and did so at least three to four times per week. Most games lasted all night and into the next morning. I can remember playing poker on a Thanksgiving Day!

During this same period of time I often took six to eight Black Beauties per week. Sometimes I would not sleep for three days. I went from 190 pounds in December 1970 to 170 pounds just over three months later in the spring of 1971.

A SHORT-LIVED PRO FOOTBALL CAREER
FOLLOWED BY MARRIAGE

Meanwhile, I signed a contract with the Argonauts. Even though the money was not huge, it was a start. I worked out some during the spring of 1971, but without the intensity necessary to be prepared to play professional football. I reported to training camp and met Notre Dame star and Heisman Trophy runner-up Joe Theisman who had just signed with Toronto.

I quickly learned that the game of football in Canada was different from our American version. There was unlimited motion and 12 players on each side, and the playing field was a bit larger than American football dimensions. But those differences were very minor compared to my personal issues. It didn't take me long to realize that I was not prepared to compete for a spot on the team. If I had been ready physically and mentally I believe that I would have become a starter.

Following some soul searching I got in my Olds 442 and headed back to Georgia. With the aid of one of my pills, I drove 22 hours straight from Niagara Falls, N.Y. to Athens, Ga., making only gas stops. Arriving in Athens shortly after daybreak, I went straight to Carol Worley's apartment and asked her to marry me. Carol and I had been dating for a year and a half.

I met Carol at the home of Bob Poss, the owner of the famous Poss's Barbecue Restaurant in Athens and a UGA icon who played on the 1942 Bulldog National Championship team. Mr. Poss routinely invited several players over to his home after each home game for some refreshments and fellowship.

After the Tennessee game in 1969, I attended a party at the Poss home and met Carol for the first time. She had come with Bobby Poss, Jr., a teammate on the '69 team. After meeting Carol that night, she and I began dating shortly afterwards. Bobby Jr. and I did not have a cross word over the issue and remain friends to this day.

Shortly after we became engaged in early summer of 1971 Carol and I were married on August 14, 1971 at the First Baptist Church in Carol's hometown of Bremen, Ga.

FROM BULLDOG PLAYER TO GRADUATE ASSISTANT COACH

After returning from Canada, I contacted Coach Dooley and applied for a coaching position as a graduate assistant. He agreed to continue my scholarship in exchange for my duties as secondary coach on the freshman team. Carol and I rented an apartment in Athens and began our final year at UGA in the fall of 1971.

The freshmen whom I coached were great. I had the opportunity to work with the first group of African American scholarship signees at UGA, including Horace King and Larry West. Horace was a very good running back who had an excellent career at UGA and with the Detroit Lions of the NFL. Larry was a starting cornerback on the freshman team.

In addition to serving as the freshmen secondary coach, I worked from the press box on varsity game days where I tracked our opponent's secondary. I enjoyed that responsibility and had a knack for anticipating tendencies.

I worked hard as a coach and really enjoyed every aspect of the job, except recruiting and scouting players. We would put in eight to ten hours per day and then hit the road to recruit. Most people have no idea how demanding the life of a football coach is.

> I worked hard as a coach and really enjoyed every aspect of the job, except recruiting and scouting players. We would put in eight to ten hours per day and then hit the road to recruit. Most people are unaware how tough and demanding is the life of a coach.

Although I was determined to make coaching my career, I was nagged by the burning desire to see the cards, and I was still taking speed. My pattern of behavior continued throughout the season, but I never let my personal habits affect my performance. At least I don't think it affected my work as a coach.

During the football season of 1971 I had my situation under some degree of control, but when the season ended it was back to the Athens-Atlanta poker tour. I am sure that Carol remembers greeting my "friends" on several occasions when she woke up and prepared for an 8 a.m. class. The apartment was often full of gamblers and smelled like a smokehouse. Some of Carol's greetings were not very welcoming. I can remember our group being asked to depart, and my entire wardrobe followed. I was a mess.

A NEW JOB AND A NEW LIFE

During the time that Carol and I dated, we had made several trips to Bremen to see her parents and other family members. We would often visit the showroom at Warren Sewell Clothing Company in Bremen where her father worked as vice president of sales. On one of these visits I had the opportunity to meet and get to know Carol's grandfather, Warren Sewell, Sr., a well known figure in the American clothing industry. Mr. Sewell and I hit it off immediately. He was a devout Christian and had a tremendous work ethic.

During a visit to Bremen in the spring of 1971, Mr. Warren, who was 82 at the time, called me in his office and explained that many of the men who helped him start the company after the war were now in their 70's and older. Since there were no young people coming along in sales to replace them, he asked me if I would be interested in joining his sales team. I told him that I greatly appreciated his offer, but currently it was my hope to play professional football or possibly finish my degree and coach football.

HEADS UP #13

Thank God for second chances.

- Forgive now, let time heal, and offer a second chance to someone.

- Learn from the first chance and make the second one work.

- Thank the person who gave you the "mulligan." Many people never have the opportunity.

- Try the first time not to need the second chance.

Peter replied, "Man, I do not know what you are talking about!" Just as he was speaking, the rooster crowed. The Lord turned and looked straight at Peter. Then Peter remembered the words the Lord has spoken to him: "Before the rooster crows today, you will disown me three times." And he went outside and wept bitterly.

– Luke 22:60-62

In the months that followed my talk with Mr. Warren, my pro career came and went quickly. Carol and I were married, and I joined the UGA coaching staff as a graduate assistant. By now a year had passed, and it was early spring of 1972. I was in bad shape after continuing my affinity for the Black Beauties and 7-Card High-Low.

One day after several sleepless days and half a carton of cigarettes, I called Carol's father, Mr. Worley, and asked him if he would talk to Mr.

Sewell about the sales job offer that he had made to me the previous year. Mr. Worley called back the next day and said that Mr. Warren and he wanted to meet with me. Although I was terrified and not really in shape for a corporate meeting, I agreed to meet with them.

I went to Bremen and sat down with Mr. Warren and Mr. Worley. After Mr. Warren affirmed his offer I returned to Athens, and Carol and I prepared to move to Carrollton to begin a new chapter in our lives. It was a day that would change my life, because I was given something much more important than a job on that fateful day in Bremen.

Mr. Warren and Mr. Worley were strong Christian men. During our meeting, they witnessed to me in such a meaningful and inspiring way that I never took another black pill and have never even thought of taking another one to this day. Although I occasionally played poker after moving to Carrollton and working with Warren Sewell Clothing Company, I stopped completely as time passed. Today, I have no desire to play at all.

Mr. Warren saved my life. I will be eternally grateful to him, Mr. Worley, and all the people at Warren Sewell Clothing Company for providing me with a new life and a great career. Mr. Warren died on July 17, 1973 at the age of 84.

I paid a huge price for the decisions that I made and did not make between December, 1970 and March, 1972. But God gave me a second chance, and for that I am grateful.

VII

THE SEWELL YEARS

O n my way to Carrollton in the late spring of 1972, I tossed my list of pill suppliers out the window and never took another one. That is the last time I ever remember littering.

How lucky I was to be alive! All it would have taken was a single "bad one" to have killed me. I had taken what seemed like a five-gallon bucket full of illegal pills, not to mention my heart had been on double time for almost two years. I was committed to starting fresh. Warren Sewell, Sr. and Jack Worley had given me yet another of many second chances that I have received in my life.

Jack Worley is a divine man. A member of our country's "Greatest Generation," he was a star halfback and tennis champion at Vanderbilt University and then served America as an aviator during World War II. His military service included being entrusted to fly Gen. Dwight D. Eisenhower, the European Operations Commander and a future president of our nation, and Third Army Commander General George Patton. He was also the personal pilot of General Mark Clark. While imprisoned for a time as a POW in Morocco, he served as a spiritual leader among his fellow prisoners.

Mr. Worley and I had a great relationship in our business involvement and personal association. I have never known a more devoted, loving Christian man than Jack Wills Worley.

Carol and I arrived in Carrollton in June of 1972. After meeting with "Darvie" Ellis Price who owned a two-bedroom duplex off the Bowdon highway just outside of Carrollton, we rented the right side of the duplex and lived there for three years. Ironically, some years later, my second wife Jeanne rented the same duplex on the left side.

Carol and I were ready to start our new life as I made my way to Bremen to learn the clothing business. The first thing that became apparent to me was that business and social interaction worked hand-in-hand in Bremen. Warren Sewell, Sr., Roy Sewell, Sr., and Sam Hubbard set the standard for all to follow. All of these fine men came to this sleepy town in western Georgia and provided great jobs and fine opportunities for so many people. The arrangement had Warren and Roy Sewell making the suits and sport coats and Sam Hubbard providing a high-quality line of men's slacks.

GETTING STARTED IN THE CLOTHING BUSINESS

The Sewell Companies were established in 1918 by brothers Warren and Robert Sewell in the Atlanta area. Roy Sewell, the youngest brother, later joined the team.

The Sewell brothers decided to move the company to Bremen in the mid '20s to take advantage of the crossing of the Northern and Pacific railroads. When Robert Sewell built a hat manufacturing company in the mid '30s, Warren and Roy Sewell continued to operate Sewell Manufacturing as a partnership.

Mr. Warren and his brothers were raised during tough times in Graham, Alabama. Rumors have it that Mr. Warren started his career in sales at age 13 when he sold buggy whips door-to-door to help feed his siblings. Mr. Warren was a courageous man of God, character, commitment, loyalty, and purpose. He lived his life to give to others and was committed to his principles, both spiritually and in business.

In early 1947, Mr. Warren and Mr. Roy decided to execute a buy-sell agreement. Mr. Warren sold his interest in Sewell Manufacturing to Roy and formed Warren Sewell Clothing Company at the age of 59 in 1948. Wanting no part of a non-compete agreement Mr. Warren bought property just across the railroad tracks in Bremen and formed Warren Sewell Clothing Company. At that point Mr. Warren assembled the team he referred to when we met for the second time. "Now they're just a bunch of old farts that can sell the socks off a monkey, but they are getting old. We need some new, young folks in here," he told me.

In the spring of 1972, I was as green as a gourd and just getting a feel for the clothing business and the "Bremen Machine," as it was called. I met with Mr. Worley, and he introduced me to Dick McMillan. Mr. Worley's sales territory was the state of Alabama, and Dick assisted Mr. Worley in traveling the state. Mr. Worley was a perfectionist, and he wanted every detail to be done systematically and correctly. He lived his life seeking perfection in God's way.

Dick was a very articulate person, and I appreciated his help as I learned the clothing sales business.

There were many dedicated people who made Warren Sewell Clothing Company a great company. They touched the lives of thousands, both economically and spiritually. Silvey Landers, Hoyt Broadwell, and C.E. "Gene" Hughes came with Mr. Warren and were the patriarchs of the sales staff. Mr. Gene was followed in sales by his sons, Danny and Cliff. Danny and I started and worked together during those years and became good friends. Cliff was a top salesman in Texas.

Robert King, Ted Copeland, Ken Saxon, Joe Wilson, Jimmy Mayfield, Dick McMillan, Bob Parrott, and Kenneth Norton were some of the road reps who made the company an outstanding organization. Ed Morris, Francis Reeves, Mac Smith, Harold Janney, James Pollard, Pat Waldrop and many more awesome people made things happen within management.

THE ADVENT OF DOUBLE KNIT FABRIC AND ITS CHAOTIC REIGN

In the summer of 1972, the clothing business was very good. Little did I know it was about to explode. A new fabric, double knit, had been introduced to the clothing market and was being "market tested" in mid-1972. The fabric was thick and bulky. Manufactured from a man-made fiber and polyester, double knit looked like plastic and made the consumer hot in the summer and cold in the winter. It would snag on anything it touched. Nevertheless, double knit clothing sold as if every American male was standing nude in the street. It was absolute chaos.

The first season that I "hit the road" as a salesman for Warren Sewell Clothing Company I did not actually travel much. We primarily sold on allocation to most stores by phone. We would tell each customer how many double knit suits and sport coats they could purchase based on their previous credit history. In my first season in the business Mr. Worley, Dick McMillan, and I sold over 35,000 sleeve units in only five weeks in the state of Alabama. That was approximately 12 percent of the plant's entire production. I was amazed at how easy it was.

The double knit craze increased as the "Factory Outlet" explosion began to grip Highway 78 from Bremen to the Alabama line. At that time I-20 ended at Highway 61 at Villa Rica so westward traffic exited at Villa Rica and continued west on 78 into Alabama. Every car that headed from Atlanta to Birmingham had to go by all of the Highway 78 factory outlets. It was crazy, and a ton of money was made during that clothing boom.

Many people believed that progress to extend I-20 past Villa Rica and across the state line into Alabama was delayed for years because of the importance of the factory outlet business on 78 West. In my opinion, that was, without question, true.

With the double knits that hit the clothing scene in the early seventies came the bright colors and contrast stitching which became an extremely popular style. During the many years that followed, fabrics and styles came and went. On rare occasions I will see one of those double knit sport coats or pair of slacks.

Mr. Warren's office was set up in line with the shipping desks so he could see all six shipping clerks. He would watch them all day and would often walk out on the shipping floor and stand next to one of the shipping clerks so he could listen to his phone conversations with customers. He would immediately critique them when they completed the call. The shipping clerks were scared to death of Mr. Warren.

One story that was told was of a short, young shipping clerk who hid in the middle of the bottom row of suits. Armed with a rubber coated hammer, he lay in wait for one of his fellow shipping clerks who would be making his way to the break room. His plan was to surprise him with a whack of the hammer. It all worked as planned with one exception. The person that he whacked was Mr. Warren Palmer Sewell, Sr. The hammer went down on the instep of Mr. Warren's right foot, and he jumped like an NBA power forward. The "former" shipper was exiled to other parts of the world. Mr. Warren was a great Christian, but he had his limits.

The Warren Sewell Manufacturing warehouse was located just north of the intersection of highways US 78 and US 27. Converted from an old cotton warehouse, the building featured solid oak floors that had a gentle slope to the front to make it easier to hand-truck 500 pound bales of cotton. The shipping floor, which was set up to rack suits and sports suits three-high, had 18 foot tall ceilings and 8 x 8 inch solid oak vertical supports every 40 feet.

Even though Mr. Warren was a very influential man and was respected by many, I always thought he was lonely. He loved to talk about his days on the farm, and he always wanted to know how my folks were doing. During one of my visits to his office he told me that he really liked how I was doing and appreciated me working on Saturday mornings when I often visited and spent some time with him. Everyone worked on Saturday mornings until noon or after if necessary. I often would stay later than noon after nearly everyone else had left for home. It was on those quiet Saturday afternoons when Mr. Warren and I talked most often.

Save for an infrequent fishing trip, Mr. Sewell had no hobbies, so he devoted most of his time to work, church and helping others. He made private contributions to churches throughout the area. Most people appeared to be intimidated by Mr. Sewell's dominance and control. At 235 pounds he was a large man, and he had no patience for lack of work ethic or lack of production.

Mr. Warren's relationship with me appeared to be friendlier and easier than it was with most other employees. We started it out that way, and it remained that way for the entire year that I was privileged to know him. I think he appreciated someone not being intimidated by him and just being a friend.

A NEW HOME AND A SON

Mr. Warren was never in a hurry to drive back to his home in Atlanta on Saturdays. On one particular Saturday morning, he called me in his office and said, "Buck, I want you and Carol to have a house. You find the one you want and call me."

Shortly after our talk, Carol and I located a small starter home in Greenwood Estates in Carrollton. I called Mr. Sewell and told him that I had found a house at a good price. I thought he might agree to co-sign with me or maybe help with a down payment. He asked me the price, and I told him.

Shortly thereafter when we next met, Mr. Warren reached in his pocket and pulled out a stack of what appeared to be a mix of disorganized notes. He finally found a blank check and made it out to me. He said it was to be used for the purchase of the house in Carrollton's Greenwood Estates. Down payment amount? No! Payment in full? Yes. Wow!

On October 26, 1973 "Jake" Swindle came into our life. He looked like a catfish to me when I first saw him. It took a few moments to see him due to a Big Orange hat that had been conveniently placed on top of the cubical by my good friend, the great OB/GYN and diehard Tennessee Volunteer, Dr. Joe Parrish. I hugged Dr. Joe. I did not mind the hat. I was so proud of that boy.

I can remember Jake riding with me on many of my Saturday morning trips to Bremen when the local political machine had allowed I-20 to be constructed to join at the Alabama line. Jake always wanted to stop and look at those "Big Bubbas" that were being used to move the earth necessary to build the I-20 extension.

When visiting the company Jake liked to hide in the bottom row of suits and jump out and scare anyone, even a very good customer pulling an order who might be casually walking down an aisle.

TRAVELING WITH JAKE

I traveled in Alabama for six years and later was assigned my own territory, which included South Georgia and part of northern Florida. When Jake would go with me on many of the summer trips, I would drop him off at the farm in Ray City where he spent a few days with Papa James and Bee. Jake would ride around with Papa James in his white truck with a distinctive brown stripe down the left side. Or maybe that was a wide line of Red Man remnants from some erratic discharges.

There was a time when Papa James supported the Red Man Company, but he was not particularly good at the spitting phase, especially at 60 mph. He would go through five to six packs a day until his dentist found a spot on his gum that looked suspicious. He never chewed again.

Those were priceless times when Papa James and Jake bonded. The young child who rode shotgun with Papa James was the same person who loaned me the money to cover my first missed payroll in Canton many years later in 2009. I will never forget that. Jake, now known as Jason, is not only my first born son, but my friend. It's a great combination.

I had to hand-pick which stores and which people I would work with on my sales trips to south Georgia and north Florida due to a rather active young son who got bored with the shoe section in stores and Sesame Street books rather quickly. I really enjoyed being in the field with customers and having the flexibility of making my own decisions. It was this freedom that I sacrificed when I accepted the offer to come inside and become involved in sales and merchandising management.

In late 1975, Mr. Worley asked me if I wanted to become assistant sales manager, and I agreed. I worked with the sales team and enjoyed the experience, but I really wanted to get involved in product development and merchandising. I began to sit in on the piece goods purchasing meetings which were led by Mr. Raymond Otwell, who was in charge of pricing and piece goods purchasing. Ed Morris, devoted shipping supervisor, was also a member of the committee at that time.

Business continued to be good throughout the mid '70s due to the next new version of polyester known as texturized woven polyester. Double knits were made on circular knitting machines, and texturized wovens were made on large, high volume looms. The new fabrics were not bulky and offered much more diversity in color and texture than the double knits. Texturized wovens had become the "thing," as did the vested suit. I never figured that out. Why add a restricting vest to a garment that makes you feel like you are in an incinerator and increase the price?

Also, trios, duos, and all types of other wild stitching were very popular. Our design staff did a great job of "creative duplication" or what some call "knocking off" the more expensive brands like Johnny Carson, Phoenix, and HartMarx.

It was also the time for Swedish Knits, a fabric that was shiny as a light bulb and was loved in the Southwest, and the word "polyester" ruled the clothing world. Business was so good during this time that I recall when one of the most immediate concerns of the company's board of directors was how to avoid excess accumulation tax!

THE PASSING OF MR. WARREN SEWELL
AND CHANGE IN THE AIR

In 1973 Mr. Warren passed away. His will stated that the company would be run by his youngest child and only son, Warren Sewell, Jr., and his two sons-in-law. Jack Worley, who married Mr. Warren's youngest daughter, Charlotte, also owned Worley-Sewell Company which manufactured and sold jackets and windbreakers. Lamar Plunkett, who married Mr. Warren's oldest daughter, Francis, owned Bowdon Manufacturing and Lamar Manufacturing.

Warren Sewell, Jr. was named president of Warren Sewell Clothing Company. He traveled an extensive territory in North Carolina and lived in Atlanta.

Mr. Worley was very involved in the running of his own company, and Mr. Plunkett, who had worked for several years with Mr. Sewell in setting up the Lamar-Bowdon Manufacturing Companies in Bowdon, focused most of his attention on those companies. It was if Warren Sewell Clothing Company was running on auto-pilot. All of us had seen such fantastic sales and profits. No one thought it could be any different, but things changed.

I believe it was after the third or fourth month of red ink in 1975 when the troops came together. Inventory was out of control, the line was huge, pricing was all over the board, and the ship was sailing without a skipper or destination. In a matter of four to five days, the three owner-families came to an agreement. The merchandising of the line, which included fabric purchasing, garment design, pricing, and every phase of product development, would be Lamar Plunkett's responsibility. Mr. Worley would manage the sales force, and Mr. Raymond Otwell would function as CFO. Warren Sewell, Jr. continued as president.

Mr. Plunkett was a West Point graduate, educator, Mercer University Trustee, state senator, and member of the University System of Georgia Board of Regents. Personal friends with President Jimmy Carter, Mr. Plunkett was rumored to be named successor to the late U.S. Senator Richard Russell, who had died. But his history of health related issues prevented the appointment from becoming a reality.

An outstanding leader, Mr. Plunkett built his own clothing companies in Bowdon which his son and my good friend, Tom, was running. Dick Plunkett, Mr. Lamar's oldest son, later joined Tom in the management of Bowdon Manufacturing and Lamar Manufacturing.

There were wholesale changes in the way things were run. Mr. Plunkett was hard-nosed, straight forward, demanding, and had no tolerance whatsoever for failure. Just after the meeting of the minds in Bremen, Mr. Worley asked me to meet with Mr. Plunkett and him. I was told that there were sweeping changes in the works, including a new merchandising team that would be led by Mr. Plunkett. I was asked if I would be interested in assisting in this new arrangement. I agreed without really knowing what was ahead of me.

Mr. Plunkett brought me on staff along with Don Bell. Don and I were young and excited about the challenge, and experienced in sales and marketing. We were presented with an orientation package that was like an encyclopedia. He asked us to read the packet and know it by the end of the week. Don and I studied the plan. We came in at 6 a.m. and stayed until 8 p.m. each day for the better part of the next three months.

I assumed the responsibility of a five million dollar account relationship that was on shaky ground as an added "treat." It was an intense cram course in "Lamar's Way" and a ton of pressure.

I was only late once to one of Mr. Plunkett's meetings. He never really gave me a "dose" like he did so many others, but I came close that one time. He believed in strict punctuality. One of his favorite sayings was: "You've got to come early and stay late to make it happen."

A remarkable business man, Mr. Plunkett was laying the ground work for the plan to get Warren Sewell Clothing Company back on track. Ironically, Mr. Plunkett, who owned one-third of WSCC, was being asked to reconstruct the Bremen company in a way that would place it in direct competition with his own companies. But Mr. Plunkett was up to the task. I believe he enjoyed every minute of it. Mr. Plunkett knew Tom and his Bowdon companies would continue to do well.

Don and I were learning as members of the fabric purchasing committee and serving on the model committee. We spent hours studying cost data and looked for ways to cut expenses and become profitable again. Mr. Plunkett insisted that the problem was primarily in the merchandising area, so that was where we focused our energy. We reduced the size of the line by 35 percent, set up key meetings with the five million dollar account and others, and formed a model committee with serious limits. A major change was sampling and buying what was sold rather than the previous "buy and can't miss" approach from the double knit days. The sales meeting was moved up two months, and advance purchase incentives were offered.

Also, Don and I met with Maxie Strickland, our designer, almost daily in an effort to make good model design decisions. In the process, Mr. Plunkett added Mac Smith to the merchandising team. Mac possessed excellent administrative and organizational skills that proved invaluable. We slowly began to pull the ox out of the ditch.

Don was later offered a very good territory. I think he liked the fresh air of the road much better. He was replaced by my good friend, Lacy Robinson. I was later honored by Lacy and his wife, Fran, to be asked to serve as godfather to their sons, Clint and Clay. The Robinsons are a great family.

A MAJOR CHANGE- THE ADVENT OF THE "LEISURE SUIT"

I had no idea what was about to happen in the late spring of 1976. The texturized woven polyester fabrics had continued to sell, and the top item at that time was the solid three-piece vested suit with lower patch pockets and metal buttons. It was offered in every ice cream color known to the rainbow.

Klopman Mills, a division of Burlington Mills, was the hot fabric line with its dynamite selling Sandweave Linen that had the current "Johnny Carson look." Most of our design ideas came from the "Tonight Show." The Johnny Carson Signature Collection was the best selling clothing line in medium price points at that time. We knocked them off like bowling pins on a regular basis. I am surprised that we did not have issues with some of the obvious "duplications."

I had been watching some new ideas being shown on the West Coast for several weeks. Fashion in clothing traveled West to East at that time, and I assume it still does. I remember calling Mac Smith from my territory and asking him if he had any calls regarding what was being called a "leisure suit." Mac had no idea what I was talking about.

Later in our regular merchandising meetings I showed the committee two styles of "leisure suits" that were being sold by Phoenix Clothing at the Dallas Apparel Mart. No one on the committee thought there was any way these "gimmicks" had a chance to interfere with our regular constructed suit sales and production. Every clothing plant in America was set up to utilize floating chest pieces, fused fronts, shoulder pad construction, state of the art pressing systems, and all the needed equipment to make a fully tailored suit or sport coat. There was no way this Nehru looking, unconstructed joke with three rows of different colored contrast stitching and collars with tips outside the shoulder was going to make an impact on our "sacred domain!"

I met with Mr. Plunkett privately one day after our regular meeting and asked him not to take this trend lightly. He told me to call 50 retailers nationwide the next day and casually mention the "Leisure Suit." We did not want to set off a false alarm and create cancellations, but we needed some feedback as to just how significant this fashion trend was.

Most units sold at that time were three-piece suits with the metal buttons in the Baskin-Robbins colors. By this time most of the texturized polyester piece goods for these orders had been received, and cutting had begun on the first of the advanced sold spring production. We were also very pleased to know we had stopped the financial bleeding and regained profitability.

Since the Internet was years away and we could not go online to check the Johnny Carson line, I went to Atlanta and looked in every clothing store. About the same time we began to get an unusual number of cancellations from the West. I became really concerned when I called several California and Arizona retailers, so I contacted a customer in Tyler, Texas who I knew very well. He scared me to death when he said, "They are coming. Better get ready now!"

He told me that the Phoenix semi-constructed leisure suits that he had agreed to buy on consignment were selling before they were unloaded from the hanger pack boxes. I begged him to send me one of each style. I paid retail, and he sent them overnight.

A soon as I received the sample I went to Mr. Plunkett's office late on a Friday, showed them to him, and told him how I had made the purchase through the Tyler store. He immediately called a meeting of the model committee that consisted of owners, design staff, Mac, John, Bill Cook, the production superintendent, and myself. Several members of the committee had already checked out for the weekend and could not immediately be reached. All were later contacted by phone.

Tom Plunkett, president of Bowdon Manufacturing, joined us that afternoon when we looked at the garments. They were very different. The garments used much less material than our products and, consequently, took fewer man hours to produce. The new competition was obviously a problem, but the immediate issue was what we would do with the production that was already sold and the fabric that had been received for the production. There were some sweaty palms around the conference table that Friday afternoon.

AN "ALL OR NOTHING" DECISION

Mr. Plunkett went around the table and asked each person what he would do. Since I was to his immediate left I was the first to be queried. I said that I would cancel all three-piece suit models booked on order and convert the uncut existing piece goods into two models of leisure suits similar, but not identical, to the samples on the table. Tom Plunkett and I had talked prior to the meeting, and we were in agreement.

Some of the committee members disagreed and said that Tom's and my suggestion was hastily conceived and ill-advised. Others admitted that they did not know what to do at this point in time. Although many of our retailers were okay with their existing orders, we could not make vested suits and leisure suits at the same time. It would take time to make new patterns, order trim, and fulfill other tasks to set production for leisure suits.

Mr. Plunkett insisted that it was all or nothing. He then made the final decision to convert the entire vested suit production that was uncut into a "version" of the styles of leisure suits that I had procured. Maxie Strickland, our designer, worked day and night all weekend making patterns.

Everyone was in a state of shock. Never before in this company's history had orders been voluntarily altered by management with no confirmation or notice from the customer. It certainly went against the usual business philosophy and protocol. If the decision had proven wrong it could have been the end of the line for Warren Sewell Clothing Company. By Monday we had patterns, and samples were ready by the following Wednesday. They looked great.

Mr. Worley and the staff began calling salesmen, customers, and everyone else involved in the sales process. The sales staff did a great job in handling such a radical change. Mr. Worley had the God-given skills to effectively communicate such a bold decision.

At first it was massive chaos. Many customers were angry and in total disagreement with our decision. Many other companies in the industry stayed with their

HEADS UP #14

Anticipate and notice.

• Look for things most people do not see.

• Don't believe in the common cliché: "Don't sweat the small stuff." You better make the small stuff the sweat.

• Be on time. Ten minutes early is okay, but being too early can be as harmful as being late.

• Use your past to anticipate the future. Be on constant call.

When you see the ark of the covenant of the Lord your God, and the priests, who are Levites, carrying it, you are to move out from your positions and follow it. Then you will know which way to go, since you have never been this way before. But keep a distance of about a thousand yards between you and the ark; do not go near it.

– Joshua 3:2-4

orders and experienced a nightmare later. Several companies went out of business as a result of not making the change soon enough.

It was unreal how quickly the design staff made the samples, cut production, and got samples out to reps. We called every customer and explained the situation and took full responsibility for the change. We had taken fifteen million dollars in confirmed orders and, without prior notice, converted that money into consignment inventory.

The response was overwhelming! Just after we made our first delivery of leisure suits, Johnny Carson walked out on the stage of his "Tonight Show" one night wearing a leisure suit that I think was knocked off from us! I will never forget how I felt in having played a role in the making of a decision of that magnitude and how grateful I am now for having had that opportunity. The response from the customers was incredible. For weeks we received call after call on how our decision had changed lives. The thank-you letters rolled in for months. Leisure Suits were selling on allotment and never making it to the rack.

In retrospect, the decision affected many people for years to come. It was probably the most important business decision that I have ever been a part of until several years later when I went "all in" to form a new commercial fence company with no money and no credit during the worst economy since 1929. God does work miracles.

Less than a year after the "momentous decision" at Warren Sewell Clothing Company, Ashley, my first daughter, was born on Feb. 14, 1977. While on one of my business trips, I stopped off at the farm and was riding the ranch with Papa James when I got the call alerting me that Ashley was apparently coming two weeks early. Despite a fast drive up I-75, I missed her birth by two hours. I still regret that, but I was traveling and she just decided to make an early arrival.

Ashley is Papa James' Valentine. She has a loving spirit and is a devoted mother. We have had some special times growing up together ranging from showing world-class Simmental heifers to winning all those Daddy-Daughter dances. Ashley is my Valentine and love. Thanks, Ash.

The year 1977 also brought a new face to the Warren Sewell sales and management team. Carol's brother and son of Jack and Meme, Robin Worley, graduated from Auburn University and came on board to learn the business. Whirl, as he is nicknamed, had a degree in apparel manufacturing and was fired up. He brought a lighter side of life to the team, and we all benefited from his demeanor.

Whirl learned the business quickly. We rode together over the wiregrass of Alabama meeting customers and selling rags. He never met a stranger, and that remains true today. Whirl was and is a "people person," and the customers loved him. He won them over with his flair for expression. We worked together for the next eight years during some moderately good business times, but the trend to "dress down" was in the wind. Although Whirl and I had some differences in business views, we always maintained respect and mutual admiration and worked things out on a day-to-day basis.

In the early '80s, trends in the clothing business became more casual. Also, a new trade agreement fostered by Canada, Mexico, and the United States, the North American Free Trade Agreement (NAFTA), was beginning to take effect.

The Sewell Years were beneficial to me in so many ways. However, I, like most traveling professionals, sacrificed a great deal in terms of the time spent away from home, especially when the kids were young and in their formative years. There were many weeks that I just did not have time to spend with the kids. I was on the road Monday through Friday and off to Bremen on Saturday to write orders.

MEETING THE LEGENDARY HERSCHEL

I did have one rare opportunity to take a Saturday road trip to Athens with Jake, now Jason, and several of his buddies when he was seven years old in late November, 1980. A couple of months before, The University of Georgia had discovered the finest football player who ever pulled a red jersey over his back, Herschel Walker.

I, like most UGA fans, was in awe of this freshman sensation. Herschel was running through and around every team in his way. Earlier in the season I called my good friend, former teammate, and UGA athletic administrator, Charlie Whittemore, to see if he could ask Herschel to spend 10 minutes with a group of seven-year-olds and sign some autographs. I suggested that we could come over during the off-week between the Auburn and Tech games.

When I called Charlie earlier in the season, Herschel had just begun his record-setting juggernaut and was still a bit of a novelty. As the season unfolded everyone knew that Herschel Walker was an extraordinary, once-in-a-lifetime player.

Charlie called me back and said Hershel had agreed and for us to come over on the off-week Saturday at about one p.m. We picked up Jake's buds, Clay Robinson and Jay Hughes, and headed to Athens. We parked and walked up to the Coliseum side entrance with balls, posters, hats, and all the Sharpies in Carrollton. We were greeted at the door by Herschel, who was dressed in his red and black windsuit. I told him that we just needed a few autographs, and we would be on our way. Herschel told us to follow him to the locker room and put our backpacks full of gear that we wanted him to autograph on the training table. I remember him saying, "Are you guys in a hurry?" Before I could get a word out, Jake said, "No sir, we got plenty of time."

Four hours later, we said goodbye to the greatest football player in UGA history. He had taken the boys through every part of the athletic department— locker room, weight room, offices, practice fields, media center— you name it. I was amazed at how much he enjoyed giving those kids such an extensive tour. He devoted his Saturday afternoon, his only break for the entire season, to spend with us. Not only was Herschel Walker a great football player, but he is an equally great person.

I did not see Herschel again until 25 years later at a retirement function for Coach Dooley at the Athens Country Club. I was sitting at the 1968 SEC Champions table which backed up to the 1980 National Champions group where Hershel's chair backed up to mine. We had a long conversation. He described the meeting with the boys in great detail. Herschel Walker is one of a kind.

THE LATE '70S AND EARLY '80S

The period of the late '70s through the early '80s brought an eventual end to the polyester Leisure Suit and to the polyester period. Both entities died as suddenly as they arrived, and the company had to close out several thousand units. By now, however, a financial killing had been made.

I was doing great in my sales, in my new merchandising career, and in my regular poker games at the club. Yet, I had no real connection with God. I just took the credit and chose to ignore who deserved the real credit.

We joined Our Lady of Perpetual Help Catholic Church when we first moved to Carrollton. Father Michael Regan, the Monsignor, became a great friend and later agreed to become Ashley's godfather. Father Regan had a menagerie of all kinds of animals, and we visited his petting zoo often when Jason and Ashley were young.

In late 1977 we transferred our membership to St. Margaret's Episcopal Church in Carrollton. St. Margaret's had been our first choice, but we fell in love with Father Regan and remained at his church for several years. Jim Callahan was our rector at St. Margaret's, and we became great friends.

Although I later became a lay reader and leader of lay readers, I never felt that I was good enough to vest for the services for some reason. I enjoyed the experience, but I was unusually nervous during the readings. In the Episcopal Church there are two lay readers for each service, and they wear long white robes with collars exactly like the rector.

Communion, which is special in the Episcopal Church and is held at most services, is conducted with real red wine. When Rev. Callahan overestimated the needed amount, the lay readers had to drink the wine that remained because it had been consecrated and could not be thrown out. I can recall leaving church a few times with a slight buzz. Rev. Callahan was a hoot. God bless him. Peg, his wife, was a great inspiration as well.

Since I was making a good income selling rags, we decided to buy a lot adjacent to the new nine holes at Sunset Hills Country Club. The club had purchased the land from E. N. Keith, and the lots were laid out by my good friend and architect, Roy Denney. I can remember riding around with Roy in Mr. Keith's cow pasture and staking off the lots. The first to buy a lot on the property, we closed on the lot for $15,000. Mr. Keith's cows were still grazing where the par five #11 hole is today. We built a 4,000-square foot home and moved in the spring of 1977.

CHANGES MOVING INTO THE '80S

Our family continued to grow as we moved into the '80s. My second daughter, Saralyn, was born on Sept. 30, 1982. Joining Jason, who would soon be turning nine, and Ashley, who was five, Saralyn was nicknamed "Princess" by Papa James. It is a name that she has upheld for the 28 years that have followed. She has been a great inspiration in my life as we have not only been father-daughter but close friends as well.

Two years later on Nov. 18, 1984, my third daughter, Kristin, was born. Although Papa James nicknamed her "Sunshine," Jason tagged her with "Krick," and that name stuck. Krick is a special person.

As we kicked in the '80s, we began to notice many changes in the clothing industry. Natural fiber blends of wool, cotton, and linen were becoming popular, and more traditional styling such as soft shoulder treatments were in vogue.

Also, the factory outlet stores that had sprung up like weeds on every four-lane in the South during the early '70s began to fall by the wayside. Most of them died with the end of the polyester boom. We were headed for a return to traditionalism.

I continued to work with Mr. Plunkett and Mac Smith in developing the lines. Mac and I made many trips to New York to purchase piece goods and worked closely with Maxie Strickland, our chief designer, in selecting model styles.

In 1976, I was asked to join the Board of Directors of both Warren Sewell Clothing Company and Bremen-Bowdon Investment Company. BBIC was our manufacturing company which operated independently from WSCC. Mr. Plunkett retired in 1982, and I was named as his successor to lead the merchandising area of what was then a forty million dollar company. No small task.

The company operated essentially by committee with all four areas, administration, sales, merchandising, and finance, operating independently of each other. The "management-by-committee" style worked fine when Mr. Plunkett was in charge, but when he retired that form of management style became difficult. We had too many steering wheels on the same bus, and no one was charged with making final decisions for the overall company.

I advocated naming a CEO with all four department managers reporting to that person. That request was repeatedly denied by the Board of Directors, and after two years of working in these circumstances, we offered to sell our interest in the company. Robin Worley and Dick Plunkett were Mr. Warren's grandsons, and I understood their desire to continue leading the company. I felt I could start a new career outside of Warren Sewell Clothing Company so I prepared a proposal to sell. The Board agreed to our proposal, and we liquidated all the stock owned by our family in all the companies on Oct. 16, 1986.

It had been a long run with some great times, and I left with no malice toward anyone. I wished Robin Worley, Dick Plunkett, Mac Smith and all my associates the best and began focusing on other business opportunities. There is no question that we sold at the right time, but with that decision new challenges would appear in the near future.

THE MEMORABLE TRIP HOME

Before leaving this period of my life, I feel it is important to share something that occurred in 1982. It was one of three distinct times in my life when I believe God spared me from death.

It was a typical work day at Warren Sewell in early spring of 1982. It had not rained for weeks. I had recently purchased a new front wheel drive automobile. It was coal black, two-door, and big time hot-looking. Front wheel drive was the new fad in cars, and I went for it.

Early that afternoon a log-floating rain hit Haralson and Carroll counties. As I headed for home to Carrollton on the old two-lane US 27 South about 5:45 p.m., I was running about 45 mph in the torrential downpour. As I started up a hill just before Bowdon Junction I felt my rear wheels begin to slide to my left completely out of control. Totally perpendicular to the highway and sliding toward the ditch on the other side of 27, I somehow managed to avoid hitting the brakes. Sliding down the highway, I looked up and saw an 18-wheeler bearing down on me no more than 50 yards away. I knew he could not stop, and I was helpless. I remember turning the wheel as far as I could to one direction or the other; I really do not remember why. I suppose I just wanted to do something, even if it was wrong.

When I made the turn one of my rear wheels regained some traction, I did a 180 back to the left, and my left front tire caught the edge of the shoulder. As the tire caught the shoulder of the road the car did another 180 and was now sliding sideways on the shoulder at over forty mph. The 18-wheeler passed me on the other shoulder, and I continued for nearly 150 feet into the ditch on the right shoulder. I did not hit a mail box, a barricade, a light pole, culvert, or any obstruction, which was absolutely unbelievable. If you ride down that highway today you can see that there are only one or two places that do not have obstructions at least every 100 feet all the way from Bremen to Carrollton. I finally came to a stop with the rear end of the car down in the ditch and the front wheels free-wheeling in the air. It was pouring rain, and the car was covered in mud and grass. I climbed out the driver's side door NASCAR style and made it to a nearby house. The wrecker came, and I made it home. I don't think that I slept for three days.

I had the car detailed and, amazingly, there was no structural damage. I sold it the next day, and I will never have another front wheel drive vehicle again. Not sure they even make them anymore.

Thanks be to God.

EVERY REASON TO BE HAPPY, BUT...

Carol, our four kids, and I had every reason to be happy, especially if you considered our financial gain. I had never seen a figure on a check like the one we received at John Wasdin's office in mid-October, 1986. We bought a 200-acre farm on Oak Mountain, built a white mansion with Scarlett O'Hara columns, and had 100 of the best cattle in the land. Our kids were healthy and safe. But things began to unravel.

We moved to the farm in search of something, and I am not sure to this day what that really was. Three years to the month from the sale of our stake in the clothing companies, Carol and I divorced in October,

---

HEADS UP #15

Do all you can to prepare for one marriage partner in your life.

• How does he or she relate to your friends? It's more important than you may think.

• Make sure that the church and a growing relationship with Christ is a key element in the choice of a lifelong partner.

• Make sure the money is understood. You should be willing to have a joint checking account.

• Be faithful in all facets of marriage.

Love is patient, love is kind. It does not envy, it does not boast, it is not proud. It is not rude, it is not self-seeking, it is not easily angered, it keeps no record of wrongs. Love does not delight in evil but rejoices with truth. It always protects, it always trusts, always hopes, always perseveres..

– 1 Corinithians 13:4-7

1989. Like most divorces it was tough on all parties. I was devastated, but we worked out the details. Carol and I shared many great times during our nearly 18 years together. We had four wonderful kids together, and I became a member of two tremendous families, the Worleys and the Sewells.

I would be remiss if I did not say something about my former mother-in-law, Charlotte Worley, or Meme as she was called. A memorable example of her generosity occurred just after Carol and I moved into the house in Carrollton's Greenwood Estates that Mr. Sewell, Carol's grandfather, had bought us. One Saturday morning I was weeding the back yard when a landscape truck pulled up with tons of all kinds of shrubs. I was a bit annoyed at first by the totally unexpected purchase by Meme. I guess I just wasn't accustomed to such generosity. But that's the kind of person Meme was. She cared so much for others and had many of the same traits of giving and doing as her father had, the late Warren Sewell, Sr.

As some time passed after the divorce I was okay, but my primary concern was for the kids. I have had a long time to reflect, but I don't spend too much time looking back. I take full responsibility for my part in the failure of our marriage. I know that I did not provide the Christian example that I should have. There is no doubt that I placed materialistic "things" ahead of a relationship with God and my family. We went to church, but for me it was like the lyrics of the song that includes the line, "just going through the motions."

I want to add that no matter what the consequences and implications were at the time, God has a way of redemption. Just think about the Butterfly Effect that produced two great examples of God's creation in James A. Swindle, ll and Mark W. Swindle as an indirect result of the circumstances, not to mention the impact Jeanne Swindle has had on all our lives.

VIII
THE '90s

Life was very different after the October, 1989 divorce and without all the "things" I previously had at my disposal. But of most importance in my life at the time were my kids.

Jason was enrolled at Riverside Military Academy in Gainesville, Ga., the same college preparatory school that I attended and that his great-grandfather attended many years before. He played wide receiver on the RMA football squad and broke some of my past receiving records.

We sold the farm at Oak Mountain, and Ashley, Saralyn, and Kristin moved with Carol to a house on Lake Carroll. Buying a lot in Stoney Brook, a small development on the east side of town, I built a house that I designed and lived in it for the next year.

We agreed on joint custody, and I had my kids every other weekend with designated holidays. I was good to go with that legal agreement and was ready to make it work. My house was about three miles away from where the girls and their mom lived so there was no problem with transportation. We had great times at Stoney Brook.

By this time I had my real estate license and was making good listings and sales, beginning with earning "Million Dollar Club" in my first year in 1990. I enjoyed the new life and the freedom that it afforded me.

There were other changes in my life, including a move from St. Margaret's Episcopal Church to visiting at various other local churches. The memories at St. Margaret's were just too difficult for me at the time. The girls were acolytes, and the Christmas pageant was always in my mind. I needed a break from the past.

Having always wanted to be a ski instructor or member of a ski patrol as a part of my bucket list, I applied at Winter Park, Co. and was invited out for a ski test. I made the grade as far as my skiing abilities. I needed only to complete EMT training to finish the process. But I began to have second thoughts and eventually decided not to pursue the opportunity. The primary factor in my decision was that it would take me away from the kids.

On my return to Carrollton from Colorado, I learned that Carol had moved to St. Augustine, Fl with my children. I made an attempt to contact the kids. I was devastated.

Looking back in time through the rearview mirror that God provides us when we are willing to honestly look at ourselves, there was only one person to blame for all this. That person was me.

JEANNE

Jeanne Newberry and I met through a mutual friend, and we began dating in the early fall of 1990. We hit it off immediately. After a short time I proposed, and we were married on December 22, 1990.

At the time we married, each of

HEADS UP #16

Stay in control. Smile your life away.

• Learn to smile and talk at the same time. It takes some practice. Just try it.

• Never use profanity. It makes you look ignorant.

• No frowns allowed. Nobody likes frowners.

• Never raise your voice in anger at anyone. Just program your radar to not engage.

• Try to argue in a whisper. It works.

When they heard this, they were furious and gnashed their teeth at him. But Stephen, full of the Holy Spirit, looked up at heaven and saw the glory of God, and Jesus standing at the right hand of God. "Look," he said. " I see heaven open and the Son of Man standing at the right hand of God."
– Acts 7: 54-56

us owned a home, so we put both of them up for sale. I sold my house in Stoney Brook almost immediately, and we moved into Jeanne's house in Fairfield Plantation and lived there for most of 1991. In December of 1991, we purchased a home in a secluded area near the University of West Georgia. We reside there today, and I hope we never leave.

Meanwhile, I decided that selling real estate was just not for me in the long term. I wanted to get back into apparel manufacturing. We had done a great job at Warren Sewell in developing a very profitable company. I knew the business and had an interest in active apparel so I began researching that specific area of the industry. Although I was very familiar with the merchandising and sales aspects of the business, manufacturing was where I needed guidance.

In the spring of 1991 I formed a partnership with a former co-worker from the Warren Sewell organization who had been the number two man in production management. We operated for approximately eight months, but things just did not work out. The partnership was terminated. **Just a mini-heads up – I do not suggest going in business with a close friend. You will likely lose money and the friend.**

During the mid-nineties I continued to grow my active-wear business and was selling blank imprintable products to larger screen print and embroidery companies. I was selling product primarily to suppliers to large discount retailers.

One of our largest customers began a long and difficult trend of slower and slower payments. The situation did not improve well into the late '90s, and we were faced with a difficult decision: either file legal action and possibly force him into bankruptcy or allow the outstanding debt to be applied toward the purchase of the existing vendor number and go directly to the primary retailer. I decided on the latter option; it was the only way I could see to even come close to being paid.

Sales for my customers had fallen below $100,000 with the retailer, and the end was near. We moved quickly to set up a new company and transfer the vendor number. It began to fall into place, and in early 2000 we were back in business.

THE NEWBERRYS

Jeanne and I have similar backgrounds. Both of the one-story farm homes in which we spent our childhoods were located on long, paved roads running through flat, fertile farmland. Each of us was raised to work on the farm and learned early in life to appreciate the outdoors and the American way of life.

Jeanne has three brothers. Steve is a natural-born farmer and knows his business, and Dick, Jeanne's middle brother, is an awesome caregiver and state-of-the-art farmer/fisherman/hunter who can do anything when it comes to farm related activity.

Jeanne's oldest brother, Bill, and his wife, Margaret, built a home at the

Pictured, at a Newberry family lunch (left to right) Buck; Jeanne's dad, Bill Newberry, her uncle, John DeVries; her Aunt Frances DeVries; her late mother, "Pete" Newberry; her aunts, Jeanne Roe and Meida Newberry; and her uncles, Louie Newberry and Hugh Roe.

farm where they reside today. Bill has helped many farmers sustain their livelihood during his thirty-plus year career leading the local Production Credit Association.

Sheryl, Jeanne's sister, is a multi-trained genius with degrees in law and nursing. She knows how to help others and is always pitching in.

Jeanne's mother, Mary Katherine Peters Newberry, was an exceptional person, wife, and mother. She was with the Army Nurse Corps during World War II and met William Harold "Bill" Newberry at the famous Potsdam Conference in Potsdam, Germany in August of 1945. The Potsdam Conference, held just after the unconditional surrender of Germany, was charged by the victorious Allied Powers to determine the fate of the Nazi leaders and to form a plan of reconstruction following over four years of horrific war.

Mr. Bill was a farm boy from Lizella, Georgia. "Pete," an Army nickname from her maiden name, Peters, was from Kalamazoo, Michigan. The fact that they hailed from two completely different areas of the country made no difference. When they returned to the states, Mr. Bill called "Pete" and asked her to come south. They married on January 11, 1947, bought a place in Louisville, Georgia and raised their family on a 500-acre farm. They were fondly known to everyone throughout the county as Pete and Bill.

As the grandchildren arrived, "Pete" soon became "Gram," a term of endearment used even by her children. She was a devout Roman Catholic and made sure her faith was a top priority. Southeast Georgia is not exactly the breadbasket of Catholicism, but Gram always managed to have her family in church on Sunday, even when the mass was held in the local movie theatre.

Gram was a dedicated public health nurse in Jefferson County for 40 years. Her invaluable service to the community included counseling to expectant mothers, home-calls to the elderly, administering medications, patching up whatever was cut or scraped, and vaccinating just about every baby born in the county for decades. Gram did what most great Americans do: whatever was needed and more for the people who she served.

Gram was a devoted wife, mother and grandmother. Always straight forward, she never left any doubt about her position on any subject. She loved to cook, and expressed her love for her family with the meals she prepared. She passed away in 1998 and will be missed by the many people whose lives she touched.

Ironically, Jeanne's father, Bill Newberry, was in the same graduating class of 1941 at the University of Georgia as my mother, Bee, although they did not know each other at the time. He served our nation during World War II and had the opportunity to meet General George Patton on several occasions. Returning home after the war, "Papa," as he is known by his family, set out to find some farm land and raise a family. He succeeded on both counts, developing a beautiful, productive farm and along with Gram raising six children, of which Jeanne is the youngest.

Bill is a die-hard Georgia Bulldog, so we had no problem finding common ground. Just as fervent and dedicated when the Atlanta Braves are the subject of discussion, he rarely misses a Braves game on television.

With the Federal Land Bank for 24 years, Bill was instrumental in providing needed financing for area farmers. He served 22 years on the local Jefferson Electric Board of Directors and six years on the National Rural Utilities Cooperative Finance Corporation Board that represents the rural electric cooperatives in Georgia. Papa continues to enjoy a simple, uncomplicated lifestyle. He loves and respects the land and what it provides in God's Kingdom. Much like Gram in that he puts his faith first and never stops helping others, Papa is a strict believer in ethics and defined standards.

Jeanne and her siblings are fortunate to have parents like Gram and Papa. Each of them represents what God put us here for---serving others.

A FATHER AGAIN IN MY FORTIES

Jeanne's influence on my older children has made a huge difference in their development. She was and is there for every event. Making costumes for church pageants and recital dresses for the girls, assisting with school projects, going on trips to Riverside to watch Jason's games, and whatever else needed doing she just did it. She has always been there for the kids, no matter what the circumstances, right up to this day. The most recent example that I can recall was her work and timely decisions regarding Kristin's wedding in May of 2010. Jeanne took charge and made some last-minute decisions that made the event perfect. Jeanne is the one who made the wedding so special.

I never in a million years would have thought that I would have had children at age 44 or 46, but I did. Jamie, who was born on February 1, 1992, has been a great inspiration to me through his four international mission trips before the age of 18, a standout career as a Carrollton High student and Trojan punter, and a general commitment to excellence in his life. Thanks for the times past and those yet to come!

Mark was born on August 11, 1994. Some say Mark is the most like me of all the Rug Rats, but I'm not sure about that one. I do know that he maintains a value system in his life anyone would want, whether it is leading a prayer at Sunday School, delivering a mission trip overview at church, interacting with his peers, or leading by example in the classroom and on the tennis court at CHS.

It is amazing how God works! The presence and influence of these

> The current financial climate has brought out the truth in many relationships. Many relationships have failed due to stress and lack of faith. Our family understands what this is all about, and we are standing tall together.

Pictured, left to right, on a stroll down East Beach on St. Simon's Island in 1997: Jamie, Jeanne, Mark, Buck, Saralyn, Ashley, Kristin, and Jason.

young men have cemented the relationship of all my children. I sincerely believe that Jeanne is responsible for that. She is a fantastic mother, mentor, advocate, teacher, disciplinarian, advisor, fan, and wife. She has hung with me in all the difficult financial times and has kept the ship afloat when fence sales were in the tank.

The current financial climate has brought out the truth in many relationships. Many relationships have failed due to stress and lack of faith. Our family understands what this is all about, and we are standing tall together. I greatly appreciate Jeanne's support during the times of stress and uncertainty. She is a tremendous person, and I am so fortunate to have her as a wife and friend.

Thank God for Jeanne.

IX

THE 2000'S

The '90s were busy for us. Papa James passed away on Sept. 10, 1993. Jamie and Mark were playing T-Ball and soccer and all the other typical boy stuff. I was able to spend a ton of time with Jamie and Mark, which has no price tag. I realize that I could have found a job working for someone else, but self employment allowed me to spend extra time with Jeanne and the boys.

Unfortunately, I was not in the same position with Ashley, Jason, Saralyn, and Kristin. The overnight road travel and work on weekends paid the bills during the Sewell Days, but there was a huge price to pay in terms of time spent away from home.

On the business front, I established a new active-wear company that began selling directly to retailers in 2000. We had no credit and little cash. This would be an all too familiar situation a few years later. But I put together a national sales organization and sales began to come in. We operated this company for three years and built sales from $100,000 in 2001 to over three million per year by 2004.

THE GAME

One of the most exciting and amazing things to happen in the 2000s was what the A.C. Reynolds High School Lady Rockets accomplished on March 11, 2000 at the Dean Smith Center at the University of North Carolina. My daughters, Saralyn and Kristin, lived with their mother in Ashville and attended A.C. Reynolds High School. Both girls had been actively involved in year round-AAU basketball since early middle school. AAU basketball and basketball in general is "King in Carolina". 2000 was Saralyn's senior year and Krick's sophomore year. Most all of these girls had played together year round since they learned to read. The 2000 Lady Rockets had a great year, only losing four games in 32, and it was playoff time. There was great anticipation, but the competition was fierce and one giant by the name of Terry Sanford High School was deemed to be unbeatable with four girls over six feet in height with speed and depth to burn. The Lady Rockets narrowly won the first two sectional games by three points each and wrapped it up with a 28 point win in the finals. The streak continued in the regionals with an easy win over Providence and a narrow, come-from-behind win over heavily favored Freedom. It was down to two teams for the "Show" in one of the most well-known and respected venues in college sports--The Dean Dome -- the Lady Rockets and yes, the "unbeatable ladies from Terry Sanford High School." Saralyn often started, but she was listed as the first sub for the championship game due to Sanford's height advantage. The Lady Rockets looked like midgets out there ever with their "tall team" starting.

The Lady Rockets were down from the start, but never let it get out of hand until just after the half when the lead reached nine points. Coach Lankford called a time out and put # 34 Saralyn Swindle into the lineup. Saralyn was a very aggressive player. I believe she had made only four three-point shots all year and was known for her defense. She was fresh, and in a period of three minutes, she buried two threes and got the Rockets back in it. Saralyn added another three in the middle of the fourth quarter. The Sanford lead was only two with 38 seconds on the clock. Both teams were pressing full court and a Rockets backcourt steal resulted in a layup to tie the game. The Lady Rockets had never led in the game at any time until Lauren Trantham (L.T.) took a pass from Jesse Stone and hooked a six footer in with 25 seconds remaining in the game. Sanford panicked and lost it out of bounds and the rest is history. The 2000 AAAA State Champions were the A.C. Reynolds Lady Rockets!

I was so proud of those girls that day, and to have two daughters on a championship team is very special. I am especially proud of these girls today. Kristin is an expert in sign language for the hearing impaired and she is devoted to helping others and being a great person. She is married to a great guy and friend, Red Sox fan or not, Chris Duke. Saralyn is a successful event coordinator and she and her husband, and my friend, Steve Hamilton are a perfect fit and a true blessing to me as a parent. Thanks, guys.

A SUNDAY MORNING SIGN

I believe that the Lord sent me a sign on a Sunday morning in August 2004. It was something that would gradually strengthen my faith and enabled me to ride out some very tough times that were to come four years later.

I was on my way to my regular church of 17 years on this typical Sunday morning. For some reason I turned left on College Street and decided to come in the back way. I do not remember ever doing that before. When I turned in I immediately noticed the backdoor open to the fellowship hall at the Carrollton First United Methodist Church. It sounded like an old camp meeting was going on. The music was old time gospel. I learned later that Crosswalk, the CFUMC praise band, plays old camp-gospel music every August. It is a tradition.

I was blown away with what I was hearing and was so curious that I just pulled over and walked in. The spirit that I saw and heard in that room was amazing. There were many people with arms raised to God and one lady had a voice like an angel. The worship band, Crosswalk, was and still is tour-quality and is one of the best groups around when it comes to church praise music.

Joy and Wes Griffin have meant a great deal to our family.

Over the next several months, I visited CFUMC and got to know the pastor, Dr. Bob Allred, and several of the members. First impressions were that many members of the congregation were huge Carrollton High Trojan fans, and everyone was very friendly. I really enjoyed the musical ministry. It really helps to break barriers and allows you to get in the spirit of Christ.

I told Jeanne about my experience that Sunday morning, and we later began attending CFUMC together. Another factor in our becoming regulars at CFUMC was its youth program, since Jamie and Mark were nine and twelve, respectively, at the time. I researched what the church offered and was amazed at the number of programs that were in place and planned for the future. We later introduced the boys to Sunday School and met Joy Griffin. The rest is history.

Joy Griffin sealed the deal. She is a master sales lady, an awesome Sunday School teacher, a premier evangelist, and a successful international missionary. It was just by chance that Jamie and Caleb, Joy's son, were the same age, and Jamie was enrolled in Caleb's class, which was taught by Joy. Jamie and Caleb would go on to graduate together from Carrollton High School in the spring of 2010. Joy and her husband Wes are special, angelic people. Each of them has had physical healing experiences that defy anyone's disbelief in our God of all creation.

Wes is a true Christian visionary, as well as an avid outdoorsman, and fellow member of Pathfinders, our weekly men's Bible study group. The energy and excitement that Wes creates in his life and the lives of others is contagious.

A few years ago Joy and Wes had a vision. They wanted to establish an international mission training ministry that would reach out to all those worldwide who have not had the opportunity to experience Christianity. The International Leadership Institute was created in 2000 and has become one of the most effective and wide-spread missionary organizations in the world. ILI uses training and a unique method of networking with talented individuals around the globe to spread the gospel. At last accounting over 60,000 active ministers and lay people are active in promoting God's word through the leadership of ILI. Some areas are in war torn and dangerous parts of the world.

INTERNATIONAL LEADERSHIP INSTITUTE

www.iliteam.org

Joy has meant much more to our family, community, and church than just being a Sunday School teacher. She has organized numerous mission trips to Mexico and Kenya for her class. Jamie has been on four of her mission trips, three to Monterrey, Mexico and one to Kenya, Africa. I think the Kenya trip had a special meaning for Jamie. He experienced some of the worst poverty in the world.

Prior to making the trip to Kenya, Joy and CFUMC lay leader Richard Culpepper joined forces and purchased the first deep water well in Narvasha, Kenya. Richard did wonders in making that well operational. Later, the first dormitory was built primarily with money collected in empty water bottles. The new building provided the means for the rescue of 24 boys off the streets of Narvasha. The second building is currently under construction.

THAT LITTLE GIRL

By the end of 2005 I could see the inevitable on the horizon. We were headed for the worst economic times in the United States since the Great Depression. I sold the apparel company in August, but the remainder of my financial interests were real estate and bank related – not good.

Ms. Joy had invited me to help lead the mission trip to Monterrey, Mexico and I had accepted, but as the holiday season of 2005 approached I was in a very depressed state of mind. I just did not know where to turn to support our family long term. I had my mind made up to call Ms. Joy and cancel on the mission trip, but I just could not make that call and let Jamie and the crew down. During those days prior to the trip to Monterrey I had actually considered taking my own life. This feeling was known to no one but me. I had it planned down to the last detail. The holidays were difficult for me in '05, but by the Grace of God, I was able to make it to the church parking lot at 5:15 a.m. the morning of Dec. 26, 2005. A crew of 15 brave souls departed for the Atlanta airport. We had a 3 hour flight to Monterrey and my thoughts were on my financial situation the entire duration of the flight. We were met by Pastor Florencio Guzman and his sons at the Monterrey Airport. Florencio had developed a ministry to the proverty stricken population of the Monterrey area known as Vina Del Rey–10 locations throughout the area that he dedicated his life to. He, and his entire family, are amazing disciples of Jesus.

We arrived in Monterrey at around lunch and grabbed a bite and headed to our first stop at a place called Aleanz Real. This was one of Florenzio's missions that had not been visited by a mission group in well over a year and Ms. Joy was determined to make this a priority, but time was tight and we had only a few hours of daylight. We rushed around and headed for the first stop. The girls began getting the "clowns" ready with makeup

The 2006 Carrollton First United Methodist Church 9th Grade Sunday School class on their mission trip, "Operation Beautiful Feet," to Monterey, Mexico.

and dress to save as much time as possible. We pulled down a long dirt road and veered off to what looked like a landfill to me. We stopped and Ms. Joy said –"We are here!"

I thought, you have got to be kidding me– people do not actually live here– no way. There were no houses– just shacks. I had never seen anything like this before. Women and small children just began to appear from the contents of cardboard, toilet seats, and old pallets. Before we could get unloaded we were surrounded by what seem like hundreds of small children and some adults. Ms. Joy quickly got the situation under control and we were in a mad dash to get out skits and program done. I was quickly assigned the task of making salvation bracelets due to my knot skills. The bracelets had to be made from a hemp string and seven beads. Each bracelet has 4 knots and the beads are in an exact sequence that symbolize the Christian path to salvation. It takes a bit of time and practice to make the bracelets, but I practiced some on the plane

I was stunned and just did not move for a moment. How in the world could a person in that state of poverty be so grateful and appreciative?

in an effort to get my mind off my financial issues and I was doing ok.

We did the skits, the clown show, and all the designated activites and I was in charge of making and giving out salvation bracelets to what seemed like an endless line of children. I was rushing like crazy to get through the line before nightfall, but it seemed like the line never reduced. Then there was a little girl who was next in line and she said to me "Quiero los partes, por favor, quiero los partes, por favor."

With my limited understanding of Spanish, I finally realized she wanted the string and beads separately. I was in a mad rush and I just handed her a few strings and some beads with no regard for type or sequence. She quickly stepped aside and I continued my task of handing out bracelets. In about 5 minutes I felt a tug at my shirttail and it was the little girl I had given the loose beads and string to. She had sat down beside me, sorted through the handful of beads I had given her and made the most perfect salvation bracelet you could imagine. She then handed it to me and simply said "Gracias, mi amigo," and she gave me the biggest hug and immediately turned and disappeared into the sea of children. I never saw her again. I was stunned and just did not move for a moment. How in the world could a person in that state of poverty be so grateful and appreciative? That 10 minute encounter changed my life forever. My attitude changed. My perspective changed. My preoccupation with my financial problems changed from worry, doubt, fear, guilt and depression to finding answers through faith and thanks.

We went on to complete a great week of work and ministry and that trip was meant for me and God's messenger to me was a 7 year old girl

HEADS UP #17

Put going on a mission trip on your bucket list.

• Commit your life to helping others. The outcome will be your legacy.

• Know and remember the "Butterfly Effect." Small actions can have massive effects, both positive and negative.

• Mission work both home and abroad are so greatly needed. Get on the wagon!

The harvest is plentiful, but the workers are few. Ask the Lord of the harvest, therefore, to send out workers into his harvest field.

– Matthew 9:37

with a big smile.

Digging footings for a wall around a poor church in Rinconada, a poverty stricken area near Monterey, was one of our primary projects on the trip. With pick and shovel I don't think I ever worked harder, even in the tobacco fields of south Georgia many years before.

Rinconada is a place that can be described as hell on earth. It is a location the government established to "house" the homeless people of Monterey. The homeless are not allowed to loiter in town. Instead they are "given" ten meter by ten meter plots of land in a 200-acre compound to live. There is little shelter, no bathrooms, no resources, no nothing. The people find what they can to build what they can. The compound is filled with partially finished structures made of every kind of article from old tires to toilet seats. We fed the people every day, and they were so happy just to have hot dogs and beans. Most would eat and take all they could carry back to their shanty.

The making and giving of Salvation Bracelets---I wear mine every day as a great reminder-- making great music, and most of all, the interaction with many desperately needy kids, mothers and fathers were highlights of the trip.

2005: ONE CAREER ENDS AND ANOTHER BEGINS

In early 2005 I was presented with an opportunity to sell our apparel company to a large publicly traded imprintables corporation in the mid-west. I worked hard for several months to make this happen, and we closed on August 15, 2005. We had brought this company out of near collapse and rebuilt it into a viable, profitable and marketable corporation with sales of over three million dollars.

When I closed the sale on August 15, 2005, my 33-year career in apparel manufacturing that began in the spring of 1972 at Warren Sewell Clothing Company and branched out into other related businesses during the ensuing years was over.

Gates

Fence and Gates

I had been accumulating a rather substantial portfolio of income-producing real estate properties during the early- and mid- 1990s. I was also involved in an environmental company that specialized in the sale and installation of erosion control products, primarily directed to residential real estate developers. I was riding the real estate wave of "property will always appreciate," so I kept on buying on into the mid-2000s.

ROLLING GREEN FENCE COMPANY IS BORN

My financial tsunami hit landfall on October 12, 2007. Our largest erosion control products customer had purchased over $25,000 in product for his Alabama division just days before padlocking the doors in the middle of the night. We lost over $200,000 as a result of this closure. I immediately took steps to recover whatever product I could. With the help of some mighty hands we did recover most of what we shipped only days prior, but none of the old accounts receivable was ever collected.

After the dust had settled and we had time to regroup, I met with the previous manager of the company, and we agreed to sell erosion control services directly to their customers in Alabama. Our effort to provide erosion control installation services to clients in Alabama did relatively well. Although we had little cash and we were factoring our accounts receivable, sales were steady.

After seven months of operation I began to sense some personal concerns from our manager regarding his family. He later approached me and said that he and his family needed to move out of state to pursue other interests. I accepted his resignation and began the process of closing

A Pathfinders meeting in March 2011 included (seated, left to right) Jerry Rogers, Harvey Copeland, and Dan Minish. Standing left to right are Wes Griffin, Jeff Jennings, Michael Flinn, Jason Swindle, Buck Swindle, Gregg Ledbetter, Doug Johns, Jay Goodman, and Jeff Watts. Not pictured is longtime Pathfinder, Tommy Greer.

down the erosion control installation business in Alabama, completing the closure in March of 2008.

While in the process of shutting down the erosion division in Alabama, I received a call from one of our developers in Birmingham. He wanted to know if I knew of a good company that could install chain link fence around two retention ponds. Our crew manager, who lived in Lincoln, Alabama, had resigned and moved to another state. I had no crew and no idea how to source material, how to install fencing, how to bill for labor, or anything else about fence work. But I knew the company in Birmingham had excellent credit and would work with me. So I told the contractor, "We can do it!"

In an effort to find an experienced fencing crew, I ran some local newspaper ads and got a response from a young man from Douglasville, Georgia. He said that he and his father, who was nicknamed Bull, were experienced fence installers and they needed work. I hired both of them and sent them to Birmingham to do the job.

I immediately began working on material sourcing and making

arrangements to mobilize for the job. I worked day and night to learn the fence business. I went on site, watched everything, and asked a million questions. We did the job, we were paid on time, the client was pleased, and we earned a respectable profit.

On July 29, 2008, Black Creek Station in Birmingham was the beginning of Rolling Green Fence Company. Many thanks to the owners of that project for allowing me to 'bluff my way" into the fence business.

I liked the way things worked out on the Birmingham job and immediately began looking for ways to attain more fencing contracts. We received a large fence repair job from a company in Alexander City, Alabama, and I sent Bull and his son over to do the job. Bull called me and said his son was unable to go, but he could do it by himself. Bull made the trip to Alexander City, Al. and completed our second large project.

HEADS UP #19

Get involved in a Christian ministry outside of but not in place of church.

• Bible studies like Pathfinders.

• Devotion groups.

• Prayer groups.

• There is an amazing synergy in group study with open, uninhibited discussion.

• Friend-to-friend works too.

Saul spent several weeks with the disciples in Damascus. At once he began to preach in the synagogues that Jesus is the Son of God.

– Acts 9:20-21

CASH FLOW TIGHTENS DURING 2008

During 2008 my investment property cash flow began to tighten, and I started experiencing a higher-than-average turnover in tenants. I noticed many tenants moving in with other family members. It seemed every weekend I noticed a considerable number of pick-up trucks with mattresses and furniture on the move. A growing number of people were losing their jobs and could not pay their rent.

As we moved deep into 2008, I began to see a steady decline in erosion control sales, as well as a trend of slow payment of accounts receivable. My previous erosion control customer had vanished from the face of the earth, as did our $200,000+. Earlier in the year, thinking that the economic slide would be of brief duration, I leveraged both our real estate and erosion control products businesses to the max. I thought that things would surely turn around and "get better."

Additionally, I began to accumulate a significant amount of personal debt, and our personal cash flow began to deteriorate. It was like a time bomb with an 18-month fuse. I was up to my ears trying to figure out a better direction for our sub-contracting company. The noose was getting tighter by the day.

THE CREATION OF PATHFINDERS

Despite the pressures arising from the increasing financial difficulties, there was one wonderful thing that occurred in early 2008, an activity that continues to this day---the creation of Pathfinders, a men's Bible study group that meets every Friday morning.

I had been considering the idea of forming a unique men's Bible study for several months and approached my oldest son, Jason, in the early fall of 2007 about the idea. Although I had the name, format, mission statement, and scripture worked out, the time just didn't seem right. I became discouraged and very nearly scrapped the idea, but I just could not get it off my mind. My financial concerns probably created the idea in the beginning, but as the group came together a more important factor seemed to take over: EXPERIENCING REAL FAITH.

On February, 21, 2008 the first meeting of Pathfinders was held in the law office of Drummond-Swindle at the corner of Center and Tanner Streets in Carrollton. As we assembled the original group and began our regular Friday morning meetings, we noticed a growing sense of mutual trust and support. The study and sharing among our members are invigorating and uplifting and continue to be so more than three years later. My son, Jason, is the group's moderator. We rotate subject leads each week and invite outside speakers approximately every six weeks.

In 2010, Pathfinders served as beta study group for a Christian leadership development series created by the International Leadership Institute in an effort to build a more effective training curriculum for Christian leaders throughout the world. Wes Griffin, co-founder of ILI, commissioned our group to participate in the 10-week study. In addition to weekly Bible study sessions, Pathfinders has an emergency financial fund to assist the needy.

I consider creating Pathfinders to be one of the best decisions that I have ever made. We have not missed a scheduled meeting since we started, and attendance has been consistent. The group has grown steadily to nearly

Bull (left) and Vic are pictured stretching wire on our first commercial job for Headley Construction in Canton, Ga. on June 29, 2009.

20 strong when we celebrated our third anniversary in March, 2011. There is nothing like being a Pathfinder on Friday morning in Carrollton, Georgia.

MOVING INTO 2009

Focusing on the growth of our Rolling Green Fence Company, I worked on a plan of financial recovery with a good, solid crew on several smaller jobs. I continued to learn the fencing business and began to quote commercial jobs after teaching myself how to estimate. I spent countless hours going over drawings of prospective jobs and had a drawer full of what I thought were unsuccessful bid quotes.

It was a typical spring morning in early May. I was headed out for a pre-dawn run from Club Fitness when I just happened to meet my friend Jim Cooley. Jim, who was in the general contracting business at the time, casually asked me if I had bid the Canton job. He said his company had not been awarded the job and that Headley Construction of Newnan was awarded the contract.

With that information in mind, I did my run, showered, and headed for Newnan. I met face to face with Chris Merry and asked for the job. Thanks to Jim, God's messenger, for the "heads up." After four months of submitting bids we received our first commercial contract from Headley Construction of Newnan for a bus parking facility in Canton, Ga. I am grateful to the people at Headley for giving us this opportunity.

However, the job had a drop-dead deadline of June 30, 2009, and we could not start until June 15 due to paving issues. The job was a 3,700-foot long, seven-foot high chain link fence with three strands of barbed wire and two huge cantilever slide gates. It was an incredible amount of fence work to install in two weeks, not to mention weather as a constant factor. The buses had to be moved on site before July 4th. Looking back now, I suppose it was a good thing that I did not know any better than to take on the job. I went to Newnan and assured Headley that we could do the job, but in reality I had no clue how tough this was going to be.

HEADS UP #20

Debt is the addiction, and credit is the drug. Stay out of debt and live within your means. If you ain't got it, don't buy it.

– Dave Ramsey.Com

- Understand the Time Value of Money and Invest every month like a car payment.

- Borrowing out of debt – NEVER do it.

- Make a budget NOW!

- Use only Debit Cards.

- Self-Sufficiency is the goal.

Be sure you know the condition of your flocks, give careful attention to your herds; for riches do not endure forever, and a crown is not secure for all generations.

– Proverbs 27:23-24

I asked Bull to meet me and ride up to Canton and see what he thought we could work out with the Headley job. I explained the timeline, and he said there was "no way" he could do it. He was out of shape, had not installed a fence in months, and had no crew, cash, or anything.

That night Bull called me and asked if I had a problem using two other guys he had met in a Christian based program. I said no problem, and we were on our way.

I rented a small extended-stay room in Canton, worked all day, and did estimates at night. I ate every meal at the Waffle House next door. Bull and two other installers commuted from Stockbridge each day. We had

Buck (far right) is pictured loading the van with sacks of food for one of his monthly Soup Kitchen runs to homes of needy Carrollton citizens. Pictured with him are (left to right) student volunteers Katy Flinn and Julia Reed, Soup Kitchen volunteer Francis Holland, and Marvin Williamson, Buck's navigator on the deliveries.

no skid steer and all the work was done by hand. I could not make payroll two of the weeks in Canton. My son Jason loaned me the money to keep us afloat. He was repaid promptly when Headley paid us. Jason, Jake to me, has been my advocate, my short term lender, fellow Pathfinder, my advisor, and more especially, my great friend. He has weathered a few storms of his own and he is a well respected leader and professional in our community. Jason has the steadfast support and devotion of his wife and our friend and advisor, Shea. Thanks, Jason and Shea.

At 5:30 p.m. on June 30, 2009, the drop-dead deadline date for the project, we shut the last sliding gate and said goodbye to Canton and the huge fencing project. The job was done on time and with precision.

I continued to struggle financially during the latter part of 2009. By this time I felt like I owed the entire world. One item of humor in all this is how well I got to know all the deputies from the Carroll County Sheriff's Department. I believe that each of them took turns delivering the lawsuits to our door. Even my labs, Jet and Riley, became friendly with them, which is not easy for anyone.

I was asked to resign from a local bank board. The local bank had worked with me for a time, but corporate stepped in and turned up the heat. I want to thank Tim Warren especially and all the other fine people associated with that bank. I had 20 great years of association with Tim and many of the directors. I will never forget Tim and Bill Johnson making the trip to Ray City on September 12, 1993 to attend my dad's funeral. Tim Warren is a fine person, and the late Bill Johnson was a true patriot and man's man.

I had become so involved in dealing with creditors that it was almost impossible to focus on a new direction. Everybody wanted to be paid at the same time. In my case, however, that was impossible. I decided that the only way to do it was like Nehemiah did when he rebuilt the wall around Jerusalem---one brick at a time.

In the midst of my financial problems, sometime during 2009, I became involved in the work of the Carroll County Soup Kitchen located on Beulah Church Road in Carrollton. As I have heard other people say, no matter how bad off you think you may be, there is always somebody who is in a worse situation than you are. I saw this up close and personal when I began volunteering with the Carroll County Soup Kitchen. The non-profit organization is a special blessing to hundreds and hundreds of needy people in our local area. It's also a blessing to the scores of volunteers who contribute thousands of hours each year in serving an incredible number of needy people in the Carrollton area.

Most citizens have no idea of the level of need that exists right here in our community. There are so many people who are unable physically and/or financially to obtain food. When I first signed up to serve with the Carroll County Soup Kitchen, I had a pre-conceived notion of riding around and dropping off five or six packages in a few places and getting on my way. Little did I realize that over 400 individual food packages are delivered to apartments and home every day during the last week of each month. Additionally, hot, well-prepared meals are made available at lunch every day during the last week of every month at the Soup Kitchen.

When I first started serving as a delivery driver for the Soup Kitchen I thought that possibly some of these people were taking advantage of the system and were not really in need. However, I quickly learned that the recipients truly need help; they just do not have the resources which many people have. I am now comfortable eating and talking with the people and doing whatever needs doing. I drive the Alabama Street route with Mr. Marvin as the navigator. Mr. Marvin is in his 80s and knows the route like the back of his hand and most of the people individually.

The volunteers at the Soup Kitchen are an extremely diverse, awesome group of people. Several of them are elderly, even physically handicapped, but they work as hard as anyone. High school and college kids work alongside successful professionals who are retired. I was greatly impressed with the attitude and work ethic of one young lady who has a progressive physical disability and is confined to a wheel chair. It was blessing meeting her, and it was great to be able to experience such a positive person. The Carroll County Soup Kitchen is a great cause, and I appreciate being able to be involved.

CONNER COLLINS

No doubt we were thrilled to have done such a great job in Canton, but after that job things just dried up. Our next commercial job was Clayton K7 school fence for Nix-Fowler Constructors. Bull and the guys completed the job on time, but things got tough after K7. There was no residential or commercial work. I was bidding from 2:00 A.M. until 6:00 P.M. almost every day. I was beginning to get some job awards for longer term projects, but I was concerned about paying monthly bills. The fourth quarter of '09 was a disaster.

One particular example of how God has intervened in this journey is the appearance of a south Georgia gentleman by the name of Conner Collins from Edison. I bid a large ornamental fence job in Macon by invitation from another contractor. I did follow up and discovered the low bidder was Conner-Collins Construction, and I asked for the job. I do not know for sure, but I think he felt my need. He knew some of my relatives from south Georgia, and I was pitching pretty strong. Long and short of it, we designed the fence, I made a presentation to the architect, and we got the job. It was huge, a 2,700-foot long, six foot high custom ornamental that was all welded on site. Bull and crew did the work, and we were back on our feet for the time being.

I can tell anyone reading this book that I have personally felt the hand of God on my shoulder so many times during this struggle and what Conner Collins did for us is one of those God given opportunities. I can not say enough about the way Mr. Conner responded to our needs. He has a reserved seat I can assure you.

MY STRUGGLES CONTINUE

I continued to struggle as 2010 began, and I tried to keep our heads above water. Six months later, the last week of June brought on more week-ending cash flow pressure. I had several past due invoices with suppliers. At this point, I decided to hire an asset based lender in an effort to improve our cash flow. That decision was met with great concern and outright objection by our primary supplier, Jamieson Fence Supply.

By mid-July 2010 things had gotten rather "testy," but thank goodness our primary customer was cooperating with our lender and providing us with some great fence work. It was really bizarre. We were paying some invoices in advance and others were past due. I had a long talk with God about where to turn.

HEADS UP #22

Integrity over choice every time.

• Wisdom through knowledge will give you strength.

• Set your standards high and never compromise.

• Be on guard when you are alone.

• God will be the judge in eternity.

Look! The wages you failed to pay the workmen who mowed your fields are crying out against you. The cries of the harvesters have reached the ears of the Lord Almighty.

– James 5:4

On Friday, July 16th our Pathfinders session was a discussion on "integrity." During the meeting I made up my mind to get things right, focus on correcting the past-dues, and not boast about the early payments.

I had to get things right and patch up some misunderstandings with two very good clients.

I made it through one more week of intense pressure, and I sat down and made a complete financial analysis of the situation. Even though we had two job accounts out of covenants and over $3,000 in past-dues, I could see a bit of light at the end of a long tunnel. I made plans to make up my lights and get the pot right.

Jamieson Fence Supply is a great company, and we could not have had a chance to make a financial comeback without its support. Chad Kearny, the Jamison regional manager, and his staff in Stockbridge, Ga. have supported Rolling Green Fence in every way possible. A special thanks goes to Steve Hammond, Pam Poole, Scott Gilbert and all the guys in the gate shop and warehouse as well. Jamieson credit, led by Debbie Phillips, has been instrumental in setting up material purchase orders for our projects, as well as providing credit facilities for our residential jobs. A special thanks goes to Cecil Bickford, the Jamieson fabrication supervisor, for providing on-time shop drawings and great fabricated material. A special thank you goes to Richard Calhoun, the president of Jamieson Fence Supply for all the behind the scenes support and confidence that he has given.

HEADS UP #23

Life can end suddenly and without warning. Be prepared.

• Life is a temporary assignment. Chapter 6, page 47 of "the Purpose Driven Life" should be required reading.

• Tell 'em you love them every day.

• Know mortality is only a minor part of a total life with eternal salvation.

• Be as safe as you can in everything you do. Think safety first.

Lord, remind me how brief my time on earth will be. Remind me that my days are numbered and that my life is fleeing away.

– Psalms 39:4

ANOTHER PRAYER ANSWERED AND A GIFT FROM GOD

After being called regularly to substitute teach, Jeanne decided to go through the long, arduous process of becoming re-certified to teach high school. But permanent teaching jobs were like all facets of employment: just not there.

But God answers prayers. In mid-June 2010 Jeanne received a call to interview for a position with the local high school as coordinator of a new after-school program. It was an ideal position for her, and on July 12, 2010 she went to work. Hallelujah! This job was huge for us! Another prayer had been answered.

It was a gift from God to have sat in the stands at Grisham Stadium on Friday night, May, 21, 2010 and attend the graduation exercises at Carrollton High School. Jamie, my first child to graduate from CHS, had completed an excellent career as a student, was a two-year starting punter for Coach Rayvan Teague's football Trojans, and received a football scholarship to play for Coach Daryl Dickey's University of West Georgia Wolves.

Jamie's graduation night was a memorable experience, but I have to admit that the night a few years earlier when he ran through the banner for the first time as a Carrollton Trojan wearing # 81 several bullfrog-sized tears hit the concrete under my newly assigned seat at Grisham Stadium.

CHS head coach Rayvan Teague is an outstanding Christian man, as well as a great football coach. He is a maker of men, and he does it his way. Coach Teague teaches and sets Christian examples for his players and coaches. He "walks the walk" when it comes to living up to his Christian principles. His record both on the field and off the field is second to none.

Prior to the start of the 2010 season Coach Teague, his staff, and players faced a monumental challenge following the sudden, tragic death of one of his assistants, Anthony Barge, who was also father of two of his star players. In circumstances like these it made everyone involved admire and appreciate the talent and leadership of Coach Teague even more than before.

The team dedicated the 2010 football season to Coach Barge and ran the table during the regular season and the four playoff games leading up to the Class AAA State Championship Game in the Georgia Dome. Before leaving Carrollton for the Dome, the team heard some motivational words from one of our own Pathfinders, Harvey Copeland, Jr., who is one of the four original inductees into the Trojan Sports Hall of Fame. Although the Trojans lost a heartbreaker in the title game against Sandy Creek High in front of thousands of Trojan faithful, it was truly a memorable season that brought the Carrollton community together in a very special way.

A special thanks to Coach Teague and his staff for all they have done and are doing for the Trojan Nation.

"There ain't nothing like being a Trojan on Friday night in Carrollton, Ga."

During 2010 I just focused on the positives and moved on. Jeanne had a job, our family was safe and healthy, we had a house to live in, our friends were with us, we had a chance with a new business, and, of most importance, we had stayed together and weathered the storm, regardless of the ultimate outcome.

My financial challenges continued. I had the sales-contracts coming in, but the cash flow was still not sufficient to handle large cash demands like the ones we faced the last week of July.

ALABAMA BEAR

The following account is much more than a "dog story." It was an event, though we did not realize it at the time, that would lead into something that would have a substantial impact on our business and, consequently, our livelihood. It is just one more example how God can work in our lives.

It was Saturday, July 3, 2010, a typical hot summer day. We were busy getting the boys ready to start school and proceeding with typical day-to-day activities. Jeanne was sitting by the pool with a friend of ours, Lori Ingram. They were planning to grill hamburgers before the fireworks display. Jamie had just left for work. He had only been gone for a minute, when he called back and told us that there was a big dog without a collar standing in the street.

Jeanne, who makes it her personal responsibility to reunite any lost dog with its family, and Lori, who wants to take in every lost dog she finds, of course told Jamie to try and bring it down to the house. He got out of the truck and lured the dog down the street with a bag of Doritos. By the time we made it to the front of the house, Jamie had led the giant dog down the street much like the Pied Piper. We gave him food and water, and watched as he wolfed it down, knowing this would likely not sit well on his stomach. We were right!

By now our two labs were going nuts, not to mention Mark's pint-sized Boston Terrier, Champ. Remembering the drooling menace from the movie, Turner and Hooch, we called him "Hooch." Hooch spent the remainder of the day entertaining us by the pool. He was docile, shook hands, and laid down on command. We all agreed that the big, lovable dog was really being missed by someone. It was apparent that Hooch wanted to be with people and when we did not attend to him he created what most dog owners call a bark. But from Hooch it was more than a bark. It was a long, distinct roar.

I slept with Hooch the first night on my office couch in our home. He was fine with only a casual check-in with that country ham sized tongue sweeping across my face a few times during the night.

The next day was the Fourth of July, and we relaxed by the pool in the afternoon. Lori and Jim came over, and we spent the day with Hooch, knowing that once the holiday weekend was over we would probably be able to locate his family.

Mark and Jamie brought kids over from everywhere to visit with Hooch. Lori said she would take him home with her if his owner could not be found. We had planned a full-scale effort to find his home on Monday, but Monday was a holiday for most vet offices, and our animal control facility is closed on Mondays. We also had committed to a local mission project on Monday headed up by Dawn and Tim Criswell through the Carrollton First United Methodist Church.

By the way, as my lawyer son Jason would say– just a little side bar– Dawn and Tim Criswell are the real deal as far as good people go. They are an inspiration to every life they touch, and I am proud to know them and have their association in my life. Jeanne and I recently had the pleasure of attending the dedication of the new gym at Carrollton High School. The new court was dedicated to veteran Trojan and head basketball coach, Tim Criswell. The court is named Criswell Court in his honor. Tim has dedicated his life to developing young men and women through his legacy and day to day example. What a thrill it must have been to have a son as a starter and play the first game ever on Criswell Court!

The second night with Hooch was much like the first, but this time I made an effort to allow him to sleep in my office area alone. He wanted no part of that routine, and I was back on the couch----not the doghouse like most husbands' experience---just our own version of the dog house. Hooch was happy curled up by my side on the floor next to the long sleeper couch. We fed and watered him the next morning, but had no choice but to leave him in the pool area while we completed the local mission project.

We returned home about 5:30 p.m. from working, and Hooch was gone. We thought Lori might have come and taken him home with her, but that proved not to be the case. At that point we began a search of the neighborhood. I drove around and on my way out of our street I encountered one of my neighbors. I mentioned the situation to him, and he said he would be on the lookout. He later stopped Jeanne in the street and told her that he had seen the dog near the campus road entrance to the new UWG athletic complex. Jeanne had Mark hop out of the car, and he went door-to-door to see if he could find Hooch.

After stopping at four or five houses one neighbor told Mark that she had seen Hooch drinking from a puddle in her yard but was frightened and did not confront him. Mark continued his search and finally spotted him at a distance in the woods near the river. We had found Hooch for the second time, Jamie the first and now Mark the second.

We returned Hooch to the pool area, and it was night three on the couch in my "dog house." No problem. We were on a first name basis by now, and I was becoming accustomed to the texture of that slab 'o ham in the night.

The next day we had to get the search party for Hooch's owner going. There is nothing like a true dog-loving group kickin' in motion. Calls, emails, texts. You name it.

Since I had done most of the fence work at the new Carroll County Animal Shelter and knew everyone there on a first name basis I called Tim Tant, the CCAC director, and told him the situation. I wanted to bring Hooch in to see if he had a chip for location and also to house him temporarily until we could find the owner. I was concerned he might get out of the pool area again. Tim allowed me to bring Hooch in ahead of normal hours, and he insisted he would do whatever his staff could do to

HEADS UP #24

Ask for what you want in prayer and petition.

• God gave us the brain. The decisions are on us. Free will prevails.

• Read Andy Andrews's book, *Mastering the 7 Decisions.* Put the 7 decisions to work in your life and business — Responsible, Guided, Active, Certain, Joyful, Compassionate, Persistent. Thanks, Andy. AndyAndrews. com.

Do not be anxious about anything, but in everything by prayer and petition with thanksgiving present your requests to God.

– Philippians 4:6

find the rightful owner. They placed Hooch in a 5-Star kennel, and he had chow and water and just chilled.

Another sidebar: I know animal control is often times misunderstood. I do not know about other communities, but in our area, each animal is treated in a loving and sensitive manner with necessary and needed control measures. We should be thankful for the work of the Carroll County Animal Control Facility, its director Tim Tant, his staff, and Bill Chappell, chairman of the Carroll County Board of Commissioners. What an outstanding facility and a tribute to our county's leadership!

I delivered Hooch to the rear entrance of the shelter just after 8:30 a.m. Lori had put in a call to her vet's office, let them know about the dog, and left her number if any calls came in from its owner. Within a few hours of the time that I delivered Hooch to the shelter, a very upset lady had identified herself as the owner. She and her children came immediately with considerable emotion and claimed the big guy. We learned that his real name was Alabama Bear.

The owner later called us and could not express enough thanks and appreciation for us finding their dog and taking care of him. We accepted her thanks, but of most importance, we were happy for the kids. It was a great day.

THE REST OF THE STORY

Three weeks passed, and a call came in to me from a gentleman in Atlanta. I thought the voice mail message was a typical "tire kicking" fence quote inquiry. I did not initially recognize the name, but I learned early on in the fencing business not to pre-judge anything. I returned the call and arranged an appointment to look at the job. I met with the gentleman in early August, and we walked over the job which was rather extensive. Out of curiosity, I stopped walking and asked him how he got my name. Yellow pages ad? Word of mouth? Phone number off of one of our three trucks?

"You don't remember me?" the man asked. "Alabama Bear belongs to my kids!"

I was blown away. I had never met Alabama Bear's owners personally until that day, but I did know their names. Although we had talked at length over the phone, I had just forgotten the name and its connection to Alabama Bear during the several weeks that had passed since the July 4th weekend. After an apology, we got down to business with a fence

Rolling Green Fence crew is pictured installing fencing at a high security youth detention center in Conyers, Ga., a location along the "Highway 20 Ride."

quote for a high security location. I quoted the job later that day, and the following day we received a call to proceed. It was a very good job that involved a considerable amount of labor. We completed the job on schedule and the job couldn't have come at a better time. God is a miracle worker. Amazing!

The following Bible verse seems to fit this episode in our life: "Be not forgetful to entertain strangers: for thereby some have entertained angels unaware." Hebrews: 13:2

Sometimes angels come with four feet!

THE HIGHWAY 20 RIDE

My favorite country music group is The Zac Brown Band. It is not because they are clients of Rolling Green and native West Georgians but because their music is great, and the violin is in a class of its own. My favorite Zac Brown song is "Highway 20 Ride." It is somewhat coincidental that God somehow found a way in the fall of 2010 to award Rolling Green 10 large, commercial fence and gate contracts that included locations off Interstate 20 from Birmingham, Alabama to Conyers, Georgia. It's the same route highlighted in the Zac Brown Band song.

From west to east on our version of "The Highway 20 Ride" the jobs included:

 • high security fence and gates at the Armed Forces Reserve Center at the Birmingham Airport

 • school perimeter fencing at Jones Valley School in Birmingham

 • high security perimeter fence and gate operations at the Villa Rica West Water Treatment Plant

 • phase one and phase two of all fencing for the Hunter Park renovation projects in Douglasville

 • all fence and backstops for the new Lithia Park athletic fields in Lithia Springs

 • tennis courts and perimeter fence for the South Cobb High School additions in Mableton

 • tennis courts and perimeter fence for the Woodland Elementary School in College Park

 • high security fencing for the Zac Brown Band warehouse and distribution center in Atlanta

 • and finally, the installation of the Rockdale County Youth Detention Center high security fencing system in Conyers

HEADS UP #25

Attitude is everything. *The Noticer* is a must read.

 • Life is all about perception.

 • Is your glass half-full or half-empty?

 • Never, never, never give up.

 • Age is no obstacle, young or old.

When a man is gloomy everything seems to go wrong. When he is cheerful everything seems to go right.

– Proverbs 15:15

It was amazing that each job was only a few miles off I-20 and near our home in Carrollton. All of the contracts were awarded within a three-month period. The fall of 2010 was wide open thanks to the "Rolling Green Highway 20 Ride."

THE FLEA GOES WITH THE DOG

This was one of Mr. Lamar Plunkett's favorite sayings, and I have always seemed to identify with it through the years. It is reality and states that no matter how good a situation is, there will always be some glitches and or issues that "come along for the ride." The meaning of this slogan came to life in mid-summer of 2011, as we approached huge jobs in three Georgia towns—Gainesville, Conyers, and Douglasville.

It was like a perfect storm. We had all three jobs, which had originally been scheduled to be done consecutively. However, things changed—all three had to be installed simultaneously! We had been on a three-year role with a solid reputation for on-time, quality work until the "perfect storm" hit us dead in the face.

During the weeks following, a declined pay request from one of the jobs (that was eventually verified and fully accounted for) set Rolling Green Fence, LLC, into a financial frenzy. The Butterfly Effect that resulted still is having ripples to this day.

I know God tests us, and I know his plan was different than mine. I admit I was doing all I could to "drive the train" at the time. God's idea was different and he put the "skids" on me, big time.

It was like starting over. I lost the two most experienced fence crews on this planet, whom I had helped establish. I lost my relationship with my primary supplier, whom I had paid over $600,000 the past two years without a loss. It was like everyone left the scene of the accident but me. I was ready to finish this book with a happy, sappy ending with the I-20 Ride, but things changed.

I had never brought up Christ on the job before the slide, but I did then for whatever reason. I hooked up the trailer, loaded the wagon, bought hole diggers, Craig's List hand-me-downs, worn out generators, and all we could find to stay in business. I took two untrained young men in dire need of work and just took off to see if we could survive.

I went into the personal trenches and did much of the manual work myself at the tender age of 63. For some reason, I really enjoyed the work—I suppose the therapy was good, and I was in excellent physical condition.

As this storm was unfolding in the summer of 2011, I received a call from the project manager of a large, unfinished commercial job we had a contract on. I had no means to finance material, due to the $39,000 unpaid request at the previously mentioned job. Somehow, we worked

A great catch at Two Way. Pictured, left to right are Buck, Danny Johnson, Capt. Fain Slaughter, Cade Slaughter, and Mark Swindle.

out an arrangement to finance the material, and I went to work on how to make two green fence rookies into top-notch commercial fence installers. The long and short of it is this—it just was not happening.

Commercial fence work is much more demanding and detailed than typical "backyard" fence jobs. I could see that it was just not working out, and I had nowhere to turn. I was sitting in the parking lot of a large school on a Saturday morning at about 9:30 A.M. in late July and just asking God to give me some direction. It was approximately 11:00 A.M. that morning when my BlackBerry flashed an incoming 770 call, and I took it in hopes that it was a local fence client. It was not a fence client, but rather an installer that had called me some days prior.

The young man sounded eager to work, and he said he had fence experience. I had ignored his calls previously, but this time was different. I said "How soon can you be here? I am at the school and we have a CO in one week."

This episode in my life reminds me of the scene in the must-see movie, Courageous. When Javier walks up to the deputy sheriff, who is building a shed, and the sheriff asks him if he is ready to work? Yes, but no tools, not the real Javier, and faith is the rest of the story.

"S" walked into my life that day, and over the next five to six weeks we installed over $100,000 of new fence jobs, repaired fence netting and other "punch outs" from previous crews, and began a plan of recovery. "S" trained the "boys" (as he calls them) and the Crew by Necessity has become an accomplished working group. God has blessed us with a long, consistent fence work schedule, and we hope to keep the ball rolling.

I think the most fulfilling part of this story is that I have had an opportunity to witness to these guys and hopefully make some inroads into their lives with Christ as well as have them help me with my walk.

Thanks be to God.

A WALK OF A LIFETIME

Sometimes God just jumps out at you when you least expect it. In the spring of 2011, my good friend and fellow Pathfinder, Gregg Ledbetter offered me an invitation to attend an event he described as "potentially life-changing." I thought to myself that was a lofty expectation for one weekend of whatever was to take place!

I had known of the Walk To Emmaus from past relationships, but had never had a first-hand knowledge of the purpose and format of the event. Honestly, and with all due respect to my pal Gregg, I just did not need to go or really wanted to go. It was a Thursday evening through Sunday night event.

In late September, 2011, not knowing really why, I accepted and joined a group of Christian men on the Northwest Georgia Walk To Emmaus # 48 and sat at the table of Peter "The Rock."

I must admit I was apphrehensive at the beginning, but that feeling quickly was transformed into a spiritual experience of a lifetime. I do not know of an experience I have encountered in my life that I could not describe, but for sure this was it. There is no way to adequately describe the experience. One just has to walk the walk to truly understand.

One special encounter was with one of the service leaders in the kitchen area. He introduced me to a book that was recently published by his wife M-A Aden, titled *After the Storm*. I read the book and it is great. Ms Aden is an Emmaus team player and dynamic author. The book is a special gift to all who select it.

Thanks to all at the Northwest Georgia Walk to Emmaus. – DeColores

MY RELEASES

Everyone needs time away from the pressures and concerns that each day of life brings, time to clear the mind, reinvigorate the body, and cleanse the soul. Each person needs time to regenerate emotionally, mentally, and physically, as well as time to release pent up anxieties and distractions. This time is my chance to commune with God and His beautiful creations and my family and good friends.

For me, these times on the following pages are "My Releases."

The Magnificent Georgia Coast

There is not a more breathtaking site in God's creation than sunrise off the bow of a boat on a due east heading down the Altamaha River in mid-October. The frost-tinged Spartina marsh is magnificent. The moon is on quarter, the tides are moderate, and the wind is calm. The terns and pelicans are diving for bait fish. As the mist is dotting our Costas, all the concerns of the mainland are forgotten. This is as good as it gets.

The state of Georgia is blessed with having 35 percent of all the salt water Spartina marshes in the world within the land absorbed by its barrier islands. The ecosystems that are maintained within this environmental phenomenon are a true testimony to God's creation.

HEADS UP #26

Love your life.

• Be process focused and the results will come.

• Find the keys to peace in your life and life issues are never as serious as we tend to make them.

• You just have to trust your swing even though it may seem unnatural at times.

• Some guy said his half-full glass was actually full--- whatever space water did not fill air and thankfulness filled the rest. Have fun and go for it!

Trust in the Lord with all your heart and lean not on your own understanding; in all your ways acknowledge Him, and He will make your paths straight.

– Proverbs 3:5

The Altamaha River Watershed is the largest river east of the Mississippi and represents the combination of the Oconee, Ohoopee, and Ocmulgee rivers. The Altamaha extends 140 miles from its origin near Lumber City, Georgia to its release point into the mighty Atlantic only a short distance from the docks at Two Way Fish Camp just south of Darien, Georgia in McIntosh County.

The Altamaha supports over 55,000 species of seabirds and shorebirds. The Georgia Department of Natural Resources has effectively managed this extraordinary habitat, in addition to all the coastal marshlands. Our Georgia legislators and governors have consistently held the preservation of our Georgia coast as a top budget priority. I recognize and commend their commitment to this area that I see as a miracle of nature.

Two Way Fish Camp, located just off state Highway 17 near Darien, provides complete access to the Altamaha River for both in-shore and off-shore fishing. Representing freedom, friendship, hard work, and success, Two Way is an institution of what America stands for. It is home to one of my favorite seafood restaurants on the Georgia coast, Mudcat Charlie's.

I remember the impression that it made on my boys the first time I took them there to fish. We brought in the catch and cleaned it there at the docks. Shortly after that, we sat down to dine on the very fish that we had pulled in just hours before. I don't know of another restaurant that will cook your catch whatever way you like. At Mudcat's, it is standard procedure.

A typical early morning excursion from Two Way Fish Camp with Mike Evans, a premier fishing specialist, quickly yields the limit of trout for a group of five at Egg Island. By the 9:30 a.m. mark in the day, the coolers are loaded with 75 keeper trout. The balance of the day is spent angling for redfish in the grassy shells. Rick Smith and all the folks at Two Way treat us like locals

While the Gulf is known for its sea trout and red fishing, Two Way and the surrounding estuaries of the Altamaha are better. The off-shore drops from Gray's Reef to R2 are also consistently plentiful with kings, cuda, and cobia. A special thanks goes to my good friends, Fain and Cade Slaughter, for all the great trips to the off shore drops.

I have also fished the in-shore flats with Mike Evans and Wendell Harper and cannot recall an unsuccessful trip with any of these fine fishing pros. This speaks for their sons as well. As well respected as they are as fine fishermen, they all are conservationists first and foremost.

I look forward to my future trips to Two Way as the years creep by.

I also look forward to future excursions off of St. Mary's Sound, just to the south of Two Way, with my former Bulldog teammate, Ronnie Rogers, old #65 in Erk's 60 side of the split 60 defense. Ronnie, an accomplished trout and redfish angler, has been a great friend for many years. He was a high school All-American at Dublin High School and a standout defensive linemen for UGA from 1968-70. After graduation Ronnie served his state, country, and nation in several areas of law enforcement. A great debt of gratitude goes to Ronnie and all those like him who have dedicated their lives to keeping our nation and communities safe.

There is no better "release" than a two-day trip in the fall to the Georgia coast when the moon is quartered, the tide is slow, the breeze from the northeast is calm, and the sun is on the bow!

The Powder Hounds

While fishing off the southeast Georgia coast is a laid back, peaceful release, there is nothing more exhilarating than to be on snow skis in fresh powder sliding down a cruiser or bump run in the Tetons of Wyoming or the Bitteroots of Montana. I am not sure what Heaven looks like, but I do believe that the mountain vistas of Big Sky and Jackson Hole have to be there somewhere.

I also believe there is a hierarchy in Heaven, but it is probably like the Georgia Dome: not a bad seat in the house, but some are better than others. Just getting through the turnstile is the main thing, I suppose.

I hope God includes something similar to my Powder Hound ski experiences in Big Sky on my heavenly agenda. I have enjoyed snow skiing since my first experience on the Levi stained slopes of Beech Mountain, North Carolina in my early 20s. I started skiing on Rossegnal skis that were 205 cm in length. I could break the sound barrier going straight down, but I could not turn those "bad boys" in a Wal-Mart parking lot!

At some point in the '90s some genius invented the Parabolic snow

HEADS UP #27

Enjoy and protect God's gift of the environment.

• Never litter or tolerate littering in any form.

• Pick up someone else's trash.

• Make recycling a habit.

• Conserve energy: Lights. Water. Fuel.

• Get outdoors and enjoy God's creation.

Through him all things were made; without him nothing was made that has been made.

– John 1:3

The Powder Hounds on the back bowls of Jackson Hole in Jan. 2005.

ski. Every conventional snow ski was made obsolete almost overnight. I compare the invention of the Parabolic snow ski to the invention of the wheel or electricity. They have awesome control and shorter length with no loss of speed– one stop shopping. I sent my old Rossies to the dump.

In the last seven years I have had the good fortune to be included in a group of accomplished, vertical, black diamond mogul skiers known as the Powder Hounds.

My first trip with the Hounds was in January 2005. We went to Jackson Hole, Wyoming. Chris New, our host and good friend, was in the process of building his house in Big Sky. Jackson Hole and the Tetons are an American outdoor treasure beyond description. The wildlife is spectacular with elk in the thousands roaming at will on the open range. Big Horn Sheep, weighing 400 lbs. walk on four-inch rocky ridges at 700 feet, and the wolves, bison, and buffalo roam freely. While at Jackson, I took the opportunity to visit nearby Yellowstone National Park on a snowmobile tour and viewed Old Faithful, a must-see for every American.

The Tetons and Jackson Hole are majestic and beautiful beyond description, but Jackson Hole is an expert ski mountain and commands respect, knowledge and planning. The Tetons and Bitteroots are challenging in terms of hidden structures, rocks, the closeness of trees, and sudden changes in the terrain. I discovered these factors first hand on the third run of my first day.

There were six of us in a tight group skiing moguls at the top, and two of us cut off from the group to make a tight tree run. Randy Garrett, our senior member and an accomplished skier, and I were having a blast in the trees when I decided to check out a bit more challenging slope to the left. Garrett went right and was gone.

For sure it was a bit more challenging! I went immediately airborne and dropped 150 feet, luckily stopping on the side of a 39-degree ridge. The only things that stopped me from plunging to the bottom, which I couldn't see, were the small Quakie trees.

I had my poles wrapped around my wrists, thank goodness, because they helped greatly in the two-hour ordeal that was to come. I was trapped on an almost straight-down cliff, all the Hounds were gone, and no one knew where I was. To make matters worse I had no helmet– huge mistake. I had never used a helmet in all my years of skiing. I was told to wear a helmet, but declined. Never again!

I was scared to death, and I knew I was in a serious, life threatening situation. At first I just sat there trapped between two four-foot Quakies, just holding on for dear life. After praying, I started a four-inch at a time edge walk back up that ridge. At first I would go four inches up and six inches down to the next Quakie. I finally decided to put the skis at 45-degree angles and the poles below me and pushed as hard as I could. It was like Nehemiah and the wall—one brick and one six-inch step at a time. Thank God for the Quakies and, more importantly, the short space between the trees that allowed me to pull up with my arms each time I moved the skis between them. Had the trees been spread out more than four feet, I would not have been able to climb out of the valley.

One hour and fifty minutes after making the sudden, totally unexpected plunge I made it to the top of the cliff. I was exhausted, but thankful. My frequent trips to the gym paid off that day.

I just sat there for about 20 minutes and got myself together. After skiing down the mountain to the nearest ski shop, I drank four bottles of water, bought the finest helmet in the house, stuffed three trail maps in my zipper, and "got back on the horse" for the rest of the day.

I never made that mistake again as I learned natural mountain skiing is a "different animal" from the friendlier, groomed slopes of Colorado.

I have skied all over Summit County Colorado, Lake Tahoe, Sun Valley, Cottonwood Canyons in Utah, but nothing compares to the Bitterroot Mountains of Montana where Big Sky is carved out like a majestic work of fine art. The mountain is challenging and requires knowledge and skill, as well as a good command of those Parabolic skis.

My favorite run is Crazy Raven off the top of the Ramcharger lift. The steep bumps at the beginning are wide and workable and are followed by steeper bumps with trees as close as three to four feet apart. There is a narrow exit to an open field that looks like the burial ground of the Volkswagen used car inventory since production began. The Raven is a beast, and if you can do that run and stay within a 12-foot fall line with only one or two stops, you are the man...or woman. Raven is 900 yards of VW inventory with no warranty. Make damn sure you have a helmet!

Our Powder Hound trips are made by the quality of the people involved. All are great guys and can ski like bandits destined for the Olympic Mogul Ski competition. We can ski the most rugged mogul run out there and still show up within 25 feet of each other at the bottom. John Crawford, our leader and master chef, always has a new run and keeps things moving.

The most recent Powder Hound sojourn included a day when 18 inches of fresh powder fell on the slopes of Big Sky overnight and continued into the next morning. We hit the lines at nine a.m. and were on the last lift seven hours later at four p.m. Some passed on lunch and skied non-stop. It was knee-deep powder and the best ski day of my life. There has got to be a Crazy Raven, Congo, Challenger, and Shedhorn in Heaven.

My thanks to Chris New, Huck Smith, John Crawford, Keith Crawford, Randy Garrett, Bill Seaton, and all the new guys who make this a special time in my life.

The Gym

Another of my "releases" is at a site not nearly as far away as Big Sky, Montana. In fact, it's just down the street, five minutes from my home. It's called Club Fitness, an outstanding fitness facility established by my old friend Harold Neal who passed away last year and is greatly missed.

Coping with financial stress and feelings of failure is a tough process. As I have increased my gym visits during the past two years, there is no doubt that the long cardio-weight routines have helped me greatly in dealing with anxieties, as have those pre-dawn runs to the magnificent cross erected just off the bypass by the Carrollton First United Methodist Church. I want to especially thank head fitness trainer, Deborah Pierce and all the staff at Club Fitness for great job and for providing such a positive and constructive environment.

I thrive on the gym environment. It is definitely a release, and I can see results from the hard work. The psychological and physical benefits from intensive weight and cardiovascular training are clearly evident. As a nation I don't think we place enough emphasis on preventive maintenance for our bodies.

Although we take care of our vehicles with oil changes and tune-ups and our homes with regular maintenance, an individual fitness

A regular exercise and workout routine can relieve stress and anxiety.

HEADS UP #28

Get and stay fit.

• Consult your doctor and know your health background and your parents' health history.

• There is no substitute for hard work. It will get results.

• Get a work-based, results oriented fitness plan and stay with it at the gym or a home.

• Fitness trainers at the right time in life are a great investment.

Do you not know that your body is a temple of the Holy Spirit, who is in you, whom you have received from God? You are not your own; you were bought at a price. Therefore honor God with your body.

– 1 Corinthians 6: 19-20

plan is even more important, much like a business or financial plan. It requires commitment and dedication, especially as the years march on.

Obesity is at an epidemic level in this country today, and much of our elevated health care costs are being driven by obesity. Each of us is born with a pre-disposition for our body makeup and metabolism, which means that results from diet and exercise can vary. The key is to develop a personal fitness plan and a commitment to see it through. Give it a shot if you are not already there. Consult your doctor, get his or her advice, and go for it!

THE 30-DAY TRIAL

There is no doubt that the sudden change in our country's economy during the last four years has changed lives in so many ways. The stress, uncertainty and personal challenges are factors many people in our nation have never had to face before. Although people react differently to

HEADS UP #29

Give Christ a chance.

• Do the 30-day Trial.

• The day you take your hands off the steering wheel of life and take a back seat and allow Jesus to drive, your life will never be the same again.

• There is a road map for the journey, a plan, a guide, a simple and easy to understand blue print readily available for a life of fulfillment. The Bible has it all—you just got to get into it. Knowledge is wisdom.

• Me last, others first—works every time.

For God so loved the world that He gave his one and only Son, that whosoever believes in Him shall not perish but shall have everlasting life.

– John 3:16

these types of issues, I believe that our background of having experienced adversity and some of the "farm time tough" circumstances we lived through in the past have helped Jeanne and me cope with the situations that we have had and continue to face.

Regardless of the past experience, there is no replacement for faith in Jesus Christ. As I have stated repeatedly throughout this book I have been touched by the hands of God in virtually face-to-face encounters several times, especially since the mission trip to Mexico in 2006.

For sure, I have never been a "model Christian" in terms of perfection. I can assure all the readers of this book that I have had plenty of "fleas on the dog" in my life. A Christian walk is a work in progress with good and not so good times during the experience. But to me, the key is to get engaged and stay in touch with the Lord.

I have mentioned how important Philippians 4:6 has been to me. In my opinion, this scripture describes Christianity in the most succinct and meaningful terms in the Bible. The verse says, "Do not be anxious, but give thanks and present your needs to God through prayer." That is it: put some love and wisdom through reading and deeds, and you are on track to the work in progress that I described. I think many people believe that they are not good enough to go to church, do not know enough about the Bible or are intimidated by the stares of unfamiliar people when they do "test the church waters." The reality is that church can be in many places in our lives.

I would like to conclude this writing with one request. If you, as a reader of this book, have not given Christ a chance, just give it what I call the "30-Day Trial." After identifying a Bible-based church, for four consecutive weeks:

• Attend the service of your choice.

• Locate a Sunday School class of your preference and attend four weeks in succession.

• Read the *Upper Room* daily devotional, or another similar devotional every morning , first thing, for 30 days.

• Read one of the 31 Psalms each day for the 30 days.

Prayer is powerful in the process. At the end of the 30-Day Trial, you can determine your next move in the process. If you choose to continue the work in progress, God will bless you in ways you did not believe possible. If you choose not to take the next step, I am sure that God will appreciate you making the effort.

Epilogue

I do not know where the next months and years will lead me as I continue to face challenging times, but I know I will hang in and continue the journey with God at the wheel. No doubt the difference in my life has been that I gave it all over to God some time ago and put myself in last place. I realized that I did not need all the things I thought I needed.

I never in a million years thought I would have to rake pennies, nickels, and dimes off the kitchen counter to buy food or gas, but I did.

I never thought I would ever lose my credit, maybe forever, but I did.

> No doubt the difference in my life has been that I gave it all over to God some time ago and put myself in last place. I realized that I did not need all the things I thought I needed.

I never thought I would have to unload chain link fence fabric at 4 a.m. and move 200-pound rolls by hand at age 61, but I did.

I never thought I would become a volunteer soup kitchen van driver, but I did.

I never thought God would direct me to organize a group like Pathfinders, but I did.

And I never thought I would become a Sunday School teacher at the finest church in America, but I did.

I never really thought I was good enough to be a Christian, but I believe I am and I am working on it every day.

I never knew God could be so forgiving and creative, but He has been.

I never really thought God's hand could be physically placed on my shoulder, but it has.

I never knew the best fence company in the industry could be created in the worst economy in modern history with no cash, no credit, and little or no experience, but with God's Grace, it has.

Like Yogi Berra says, "It ain't over till it's over." It ain't over yet, and, with God's continued help along the way, we will continue the journey.

PAINTING BY STEVE PENLEY

ACKNOWLEDGEMENTS

I t has been my pleasure to write this memoir. I greatly appreciate everyone who has taken the time to read it.

I want to especially thank my friend, Dan Minish, for his work and time spent on this project. Dan is spiritual leader in our community, a fellow Pathfinder, Soup Kitchen volunteer, and someone who places others first in his life. Dan has spent countless hours arranging and editing the manuscript, as well as handling original picture development and location.

It is amazing how important seemingly small things like a lunch experience with Dan Minish and the best football player in Carrollton football history, my buddy, Harvey Copeland, can be. The three of us meet often and just relate to each other. Dan has been a great inspiration and facilitator to Harvey, a 48-episode survivor of chemotherapy and radiation. There is no doubt that Harvey Copeland is the "fighter of all fighters," and Dan Minish typifies the meaning of true friendship. Thanks guys.

I also want to express my sincere gratitude to my family, all my friends, coaches, mentors, fellow Pathfinders, and all those people who did not give up on me and have supported me through a difficult, but fulfilling, journey.

I also want to thank my wife, Jeanne, for her time and contributions in fine-tuning the rough draft manuscript. She has a special talent for organization and arrangement. Thanks for the guidance and expression. A special thanks to my sister, Diane for her guidance and advice concerning the content analysis and accuracy of the book. I appreciate the input and the support of all my children from the inception of the idea for the book to its finality. I am also thankful to Lisa and Gregg Ledbetter for their support and input into the manuscript. A special thanks to my great friend and supporter, Rev. Tommy Greer. Tommy has inspired many people in his life with his uncanny oratory in the pulpit and problem solving skills at the mediation table. I appreciate his advice and candid analysis of the manuscript especially in the beginning stages.

Special thanks go to Loran Smith and Chris Martin for publishing the book. It has been a pleasure to work with these fine professionals.

And to my friend, fellow Pathfinder, nationally acclaimed artist, and, of most importance, great American, for allowing me to use his painting of Jesus Christ, Steve Penley.

I also want to express my sincere gratitude to my family, all my friends, coaches, mentors, fellow Pathfinders, and all those people who did not give up on me and have supported me through a difficult, but fulfilling journey.

Additionally, I want to thank the 16 general contractors who have awarded Rolling Green Fence commercial contracts, as well as the 45 residential clients who have contracted with us to provide fencing services during the past two years. As our fence installation business developed, Tim Johnson joined our team as a supervisor and project manager and has been an integral part of our field operations. Tim is a true professional and good friend as well. Thanks, Tim.

To all of you, thanks for giving it a go.

Buck Swindle

www.ingramcontent.com/pod-product-compliance
Lightning Source LLC
LaVergne TN
LVHW011222080426
835509LV00005B/274